LIFTED

Devotions from a Heart That Chose to Rise
A 50-Devotional Journey of Restoration and Renewal

by
Monee D. Correll

Psalm 25:5 Press
Mooresville, North Carolina

"Guide me in your truth and teach me, for you are God my
Savior, and my hope is in you all day long."
— Psalm 25:5 (NIV)

Copyright

LIFTED
Devotions from a Heart That Chose to Rise
A 50-Devotional Journey of Restoration and Renewal

Cover design by Monee D. Correll
Edited and formatted with assistance from ChatGPT
(OpenAI)

Published by Psalm 25:5 Press
Mooresville, North Carolina

Printed in the United States of America

ISBN: 979-8-9936302-0-5

Dedication

For every heart that has felt too weary to rise,
too broken to believe,
and yet still whispers, "Lord, lift me."
This is for you.

———————— † ————————

Acknowledgements

To my kids — thank you for never punishing or condemning me for being the best mother I knew how to be, even when I fell short. You loved me through my growing pains and gave me grace when I didn't deserve it. You are living proof that God can redeem every chapter of a story — even the ones that start with broken beginnings.

To Brotatorchip, Sistatorchip, and Petitochip — thank you for taking in a stray and not giving up on her. You saw something worth saving long before I did.

To Momma G and Aunt Linda — thank you for taking in a big bundle of trouble and showering her with the kind of unconditional love that can only come from God's own heart.

To Uncle Stan — thank you for being a lighthouse and an anchor in some of my darkest storms. You reminded me that even when the waves crashed hard, there was always solid ground somewhere beneath my feet.

To Momma — for praying for me, and for this moment, even with your last breath.

I love you all more than words could ever express.

Because of you, I learned what it truly means to be lifted.

———————— † ————————

When You're...

Struggling with Yourself

Struggling with Fear

Wrestling with Anger

Let Down By Others

Lost In Doubt

Struggling to Trust

Needing Strength to Keep Going

Needing Peace and Joy Restored

Facing Heavy Storms

Learning to Walk Free

Needing to Breathe Again

Introduction

There was a time when I didn't know if I'd ever rise again. Life had knocked the wind out of me more times than I could count, and I was tired — tired of fighting, tired of pretending, tired of trying to keep it all together. Then one day, I met the One who didn't ask me to keep it together. He just asked me to come.

This devotional was born out of that moment — out of a heart that had been shattered, rescued, and redeemed. These devotionals aren't written from a mountaintop; they're written from the climb. They come from nights of tears, seasons of silence, and moments when the only prayer I could manage was, "Help me, Lord."

Each devotional in this book was written with one purpose in mind: to remind you that you're not alone in the battle. Whether you're struggling with shame, fear, or loss — or simply trying to hold on to your faith — God sees you. He hasn't forgotten you. And He is ready to lift you, too.

This book isn't designed to be read in order or even in one sitting. It's meant to be situational — a companion for the moments when life feels heavy and you need a word for right now. Maybe today you're battling pride or loneliness, maybe tomorrow it'll be anxiety or weariness. Each page is a hand extended from someone who's been there, reaching back to help pull you a little closer to hope.

You'll notice that each devotional follows a simple pattern —

Scripture, reflection, takeaway, reflection question, and prayer. I wanted it to be both reflective and practical. My prayer is that as you journey through these pages, you'll not only find comfort, but conviction, courage, and clarity.

I don't have all the answers. I'm still learning, still growing, still surrendering. But if there's one thing I know for sure, it's this: God doesn't waste pain. He redeems it. Every scar, every tear, every stumble — they all tell the story of His mercy.

So wherever you are, take a deep breath. You made it this far. And maybe, just maybe, that's half the battle.

Let's rise together.

Monee D. Correll
Psalm 25:5 Press

———————————— † ————————————

When You're Struggling with Yourself

Sometimes the hardest person to face is the one in the mirror. The battle within can take on many shapes — pride that hides our pain, shame that silences our joy, guilt that chains us to the past, or weariness that drains our hope. These quiet struggles often go unseen by others, yet they can feel louder than anything happening around us.

But God sees every hidden wrestle and meets us there — not with condemnation, but with compassion. He whispers truth into the noise, reminding us that His grace is stronger than our self-doubt, and His mercy is deeper than our mistakes. When we turn toward Him, even our inner battles can become holy ground — the place where surrender gives birth to freedom.

These devotions walk through the tender spaces of the heart — the moments when you're hardest on yourself, when your faith feels tired, or when you simply don't know how to begin again. Here, you'll find that His strength is steady, His love is patient, and His hands are still reaching to lift you higher than your own striving ever could.

———————————————— † ————————————————

1. Pride

"When pride comes, then comes disgrace, but with humility comes wisdom." - *Proverbs 11:2 (NIV)*
"Pride brings a person low, but the lowly in spirit gain honor." - *Proverbs 29:23 (NIV)*
"God opposes the proud but shows favor to the humble." - *James 4:6 (NIV)*
"Humble yourselves before the Lord, and He will lift you up." - *James 4:10 (NIV)*

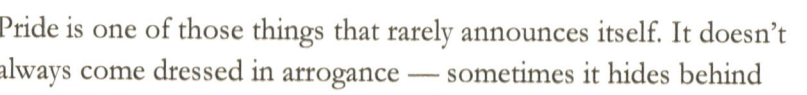

Pride is one of those things that rarely announces itself. It doesn't always come dressed in arrogance — sometimes it hides behind strength, independence, or even insecurity. It whispers, "I've got this," when we really don't. It resists correction, avoids vulnerability, and refuses to admit weakness.

The thing about pride is that it doesn't just lift us up — it separates us. It puts distance between us and God, and between us and others. When we're too proud to admit we need help, to apologize, or to surrender control, we start building walls we were never meant to live behind.

Pride can look like confidence, but often it's just fear wearing armor. Sometimes it's fear of being hurt again, fear of looking weak, or fear of being overlooked. But pride doesn't protect us — it isolates us.

When I think about pride, I picture a person standing on a stool trying to make themselves taller than everyone else — including God. For a moment, it works; you feel elevated, stronger, in control. But the stool wobbles. It's unstable. And when it falls, it doesn't just bruise your ego — it reminds you how fragile self-reliance really is.

Proverbs 11:2 reminds us that "when pride comes, then comes disgrace, but with humility comes wisdom." And Proverbs 29:23 adds that "pride brings a person low, but the lowly in spirit gain honor." God doesn't shame us when we fall — He uses the fall to remind us that humility is where real strength begins. Pride may build fast, but humility builds strong. It takes humility to say, "I was wrong." It takes humility to let go, to apologize first, to depend fully on God.

The enemy loves to twist pride into something admirable — "You're strong. You don't need anyone. You've got this." But James 4:6 tells us that God actually opposes the proud. Why? Because pride keeps us from the very thing He desires most — relationship. We can't be full of ourselves and full of Him at the same time.

Humility isn't weakness — it's surrender. It's saying, "God, I don't have to have all the answers because I trust that You do." The moment we stop striving to be enough on our own, God steps in and shows us that He already is.

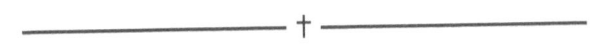

Takeaway

Pride isolates; humility restores. The higher you try to climb on your own, the farther you fall. But when you bow low before God, He's the one who lifts you up.

Question for Reflection

Where has pride — whether loud or quiet — kept you from surrendering to God or connecting honestly with others? What would it look like to choose humility instead?

Prayer

Lord, I admit that pride sometimes hides in my heart. It shows up when I try to handle things on my own, when I don't want to ask for help, or when I fear being seen as weak. Forgive me for the times I've trusted my strength over Yours. Teach me to walk in humility — not thinking less of myself, but thinking of myself less. Help me to depend fully on You, knowing that true strength is found in surrender. Amen.

———————————— † ————————————

2. Shame - Past Actions

"Do not be afraid; you will not be put to shame. Do not fear disgrace; you will not be humiliated." - *Isaiah 54:4 (NIV)*
"Those who look to Him are radiant; their faces are never covered with shame." - *Psalm 34:5 (NIV)*
"There is now no condemnation for those who are in Christ Jesus." - *Romans 8:1 (NIV)*
"As far as the east is from the west, so far has He removed our transgressions from us." - *Psalm 103:12 (NIV)*

---------------- † ----------------

Shame is a heavy chain that loves to disguise itself as guilt. But while guilt says, "I did something wrong," shame says, "I am something wrong." It's the quiet whisper that reminds you of every failure, every bad decision, every moment you wish you could undo.

Personal shame clings to the past like a shadow, convincing you that what you've done will always define you. It makes you believe that forgiveness is for others, not for you — that somehow, your mistake was the one that went too far.

But that's not how God works. Romans 8:1 tells us, "There is now no condemnation for those who are in Christ Jesus." None. Not partial forgiveness, not probationary grace — none.

When I think about shame, I picture a person dragging an old suitcase everywhere they go. It's worn, heavy, and full of things they should've let go of long ago. God's already tried to take it, but they grip the handle tightly — afraid to open it, afraid to let it go, afraid to believe they're free to walk without it. That's what shame does — it convinces you that letting go means forgetting, when really, it means forgiving yourself the way God already has.

I'm not gonna lie — before I was rescued, I did some things I wasn't proud of. Like sleeping around with inappropriate men or being someone's side piece for example. Sound familiar? But after I was rescued, I no longer carried the shame of those moments. A lot of people would have erased that person from their social media, deleting the reminders of who they used to be. But I didn't. That person no longer exists — but I hold no shame from the things that person did. I keep those memories there to remind me of how far I've come — all thanks to the grace and love of God.

Isaiah 54:4 declares, "Do not be afraid; you will not be put to shame." God's Word doesn't just comfort us — it redefines us. The enemy may try to remind you of who you were, but God reminds you of who you are: forgiven, restored, and radiant in His light.

Psalm 34:5 promises that "those who look to Him are radiant; their faces are never covered with shame." When you turn your gaze from your past to your Savior, the light of His mercy outshines the darkness of your regret. Shame loses its power when you stop rehearsing your mistakes and start remembering your redemption.

You are not what you've done — you are who He says you are. And He says you're forgiven, loved, chosen, and made new.

———————————— † ————————————

Takeaway

God's grace doesn't just cover your shame — it removes it. The moment you accept His forgiveness, your past loses the right to define your future.

Question for Reflection

What "suitcase" of shame have you been carrying around? What would it look like to finally set it down at Jesus' feet and walk away free?

Prayer

Lord, I've carried the weight of my mistakes for too long. I've let shame tell me who I am instead of listening to Your truth. Forgive me for holding onto what You've already forgiven. Help me to release the past and accept the freedom You've given me. Teach me to walk in grace, remembering that my story doesn't end with failure — it ends with redemption. Thank You for taking my shame and replacing it with purpose. Amen.

3. Shame - Identity-Based

"I praise You because I am fearfully and wonderfully made; Your works are wonderful, I know that full well." - *Psalm 139:14 (NIV)*

"See, I have engraved you on the palms of My hands." - *Isaiah 49:16 (NIV)*

"But you are a chosen people, a royal priesthood, a holy nation, God's special possession, that you may declare the praises of Him who called you out of darkness into His wonderful light." - *1 Peter 2:9 (NIV)*

"For we are God's handiwork, created in Christ Jesus to do good works, which God prepared in advance for us to do." - *Ephesians 2:10 (NIV)*

———————————— † ————————————

Some shame doesn't come from what we've done — it comes from what we've believed. The enemy knows if he can't trap you with guilt from your past, he'll try to convince you that you're unworthy of love in the present.

Identity-based shame whispers, "You're not enough." Not smart enough. Not spiritual enough. Not lovable enough. It convinces you that everyone else belongs except you — that somehow, God's promises were meant for others but skipped over your name.

But shame is a liar, and its favorite weapon is distortion. It twists your reflection until you can't see the image of God in yourself anymore. Yet even when we can't see it, God's fingerprints never leave His creation. Isaiah 49:16 says, "See, I have engraved you on the palms of My hands." That means you are permanent — not disposable, not replaceable, not forgotten.

When I think about identity-based shame, I picture a mirror covered in dirt and dust. The reflection is still there, but it's hidden beneath layers of lies — words spoken over you, wounds that never healed, comparisons that cut deep. God doesn't break the mirror; He cleans it. He gently wipes away the buildup of shame until you can finally see what He's seen all along — His image in you.

Psalm 139:14 reminds us, "I am fearfully and wonderfully made." You were created with intention, not accident. Every feature, every gift, every part of your story was designed with purpose. The enemy will always try to convince you otherwise, because he knows that if you ever truly believe who you are in Christ, you'll live with power and peace he can't touch.

1 Peter 2:9 says you are "a chosen people, a royal priesthood, God's special possession." That means your worth isn't earned — it's inherited. Your identity isn't something you achieve; it's something you receive.

Ephesians 2:10 calls you God's handiwork — His masterpiece. Not a mistake, not an afterthought. A masterpiece.

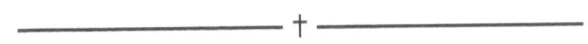

Takeaway

You don't have to earn your worth or hide your scars. The same hands that formed you are the ones that hold you — and nothing you've been through can erase His design.

Question for Reflection

What lies about your worth or identity have you been believing? What truth from God's Word can you replace them with today?

Prayer

Lord, I confess that I've believed lies about who I am — that I'm unworthy, unlovable, or not enough. But You say I'm chosen, redeemed, and wonderfully made. Help me to see myself the way You see me. Wipe away the dust of shame that's clouded my reflection, and let me walk in the confidence of being Your creation. Thank You for calling me Yours — even when I couldn't see my own value. Amen.

———————— † ————————

4. Guilt

"Therefore, there is now no condemnation for those who are in Christ Jesus." - *Romans 8:1 (NIV)*

"If our hearts condemn us, we know that God is greater than our hearts, and He knows everything." - *1 John 3:20 (NIV)*

"Cast all your anxiety on Him because He cares for you." - *1 Peter 5:7 (NIV)*

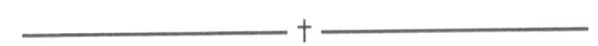

Guilt has a way of creeping in quietly and taking up permanent residence in our hearts — especially for parents.

One of my biggest struggles as a mother has been the guilt I carry for all the mistakes I think I made, all the wrongs I've replayed in my mind, all the ways I feel like I didn't measure up to the "Mom" I was supposed to be.

I've wrestled with thoughts like:
I should've done more.
I should've given them a better life.
I should've been stronger, happier, more patient — more everything.

For a long time, that guilt consumed me. I beat myself up daily for trying to save myself from depression — not realizing that, in doing so, I was actually trying to preserve what little of me I had left to give.

Eventually, after being rescued by God, I began to see things differently.

I came to accept that I did the best I could with what I had at the time. That sometimes, the hard decisions — like letting their father be the primary custodial parent — weren't about failure, but love. They were choices made for my children's best interests, even when others didn't understand.

People may have looked down on me for it, but God saw my heart. He knew the truth behind my tears.

Today, my children are adults, forging their own paths. And I've had to learn a truth that both hurts and heals:
How they treat me — and it isn't always the most loving — isn't about what I did or didn't do as their mother. It's about their own insecurities, their own battles, their own walk with God.

And as much as I want to fix it, to make it right, to undo what can't be undone — I can't.

This is their journey now.

My job is to love them, pray for them, and trust that the same God who rescued me will meet them in their own time.

Romans 8:1 reminds us, "There is now no condemnation for those who are in Christ Jesus." That includes the guilt we heap on ourselves.

God doesn't hold our past over our heads — so why do we?

If you're carrying guilt today — as a parent, a partner, a friend, or simply as a human who feels they should've done better — let this truth sink in:

You did the best you could with what you knew then.
And even if you didn't, grace covers what guilt can't.
Guilt looks backward, but grace always looks forward.

Your worth as a mother, father, or child of God isn't determined by your perfection — it's defined by His mercy.

———————— † ————————

Takeaway

Guilt is a heavy chain, but grace is the key. When you surrender your guilt to God, He doesn't just forgive — He frees.

Question for Reflection

What guilt are you still holding onto that God has already forgiven? What would it look like to finally release it?

———————————— † ————————————

Prayer

Father, You know the guilt I've carried — the what-ifs, the regrets, the mistakes that replay in my mind. Help me to release them into Your hands. Remind me that there is no condemnation in You, only grace. Heal the places where guilt has taken root and replace them with peace. And Lord, watch over my children — meet them where they are and guide them toward You, just as You did for me. Amen.

———————————— † ————————————

5. Jealousy / Comparison

"For where you have envy and selfish ambition, there you find disorder and every evil practice." - *James 3:16 (NIV)*

"A heart at peace gives life to the body, but envy rots the bones." - *Proverbs 14:30 (NIV)*

"Let us not become conceited, provoking and envying each other." - *Galatians 5:26 (NIV)*

"Each one should test their own actions. Then they can take pride in themselves alone, without comparing themselves to someone else." - *Galatians 6:4 (NIV)*

———————— † ————————

Jealousy and comparison are quiet thieves. They slip in when we glance sideways at someone else's life and wonder why ours doesn't look the same. We don't set out to compare—but somehow, we start keeping score: who has the better job, the happier marriage, the bigger home, the more visible blessings.

But jealousy isn't really about *them*—it's about what we believe we're missing.

When I think about jealousy, I picture a runner trying to win a race while constantly looking into the next lane. The more they look around, the slower they move, the more off-balance they become. Before long, they've drifted from their course—not because they couldn't win, but because they lost focus. God didn't design your race to look like anyone else's, and when you measure your progress by someone else's pace, you lose sight of your own purpose.

James 3:16 warns, "For where you have envy and selfish ambition, there you find disorder and every evil practice." Jealousy doesn't just create chaos in relationships—it creates turmoil in the soul. It replaces peace with pressure and gratitude with grief, convincing you that what God gave you isn't enough.

Proverbs 14:30 reminds us, "A heart at peace gives life to the body, but envy rots the bones." Jealousy doesn't just damage relationships—it drains your joy, corrodes your contentment, and clouds your gratitude. But envy loses its grip when you remember that God's blessings aren't limited. Someone else being blessed doesn't mean there's less available for you.

Jealousy begins with comparison but ends in discontentment. The antidote is gratitude—thanking God for what you *do* have instead of resenting what you don't. Gratitude shifts your focus from "Why not me?" to "Thank You, Lord, for being faithful to me."

Galatians 6:4 encourages us to "test our own actions," to focus on our own growth and obedience instead of measuring them against others. When your eyes return to God instead of people, peace comes back to your heart, and purpose returns to your steps.

—————————— † ——————————

Takeaway:
Comparison distracts you from your calling; jealousy distorts your joy. Contentment begins when you celebrate what God is doing in your lane and trust that He's working all things together—even the unseen ones.

Question for Reflection:
Where have you been comparing your life, gifts, or journey to someone else's? What's one thing you can thank God for in your own life today instead?

—————————— † ——————————

Prayer:

Lord, forgive me for the moments I've compared myself to others and lost sight of Your plan for me. Teach me to celebrate others' blessings without questioning my own worth. Fill my heart with peace where envy once lived, and replace comparison with contentment. Remind me that Your timing is perfect and that You've written my story with just as much care as anyone else's. Help me to run my race with gratitude and joy. Amen.

———————— † ————————

When You're Struggling with Fear

Fear wears many faces — anxiety, worry, control, even perfectionism. It whispers lies about the future, about failure, and sometimes, even about God's faithfulness. But at its core, fear is just faith turned inside out — believing more in what could go wrong than in the One who makes all things right.

God doesn't shame us for being afraid; He invites us to trust Him in the middle of it. Whether it's fear of the unknown, fear of falling short, or fear of letting go, His Word reminds us that peace doesn't come from knowing the outcome — it comes from knowing Who's in control.

These devotions walk through the many shades of fear we face and the unshakable truth that even when we're trembling, we're still held. Because courage isn't the absence of fear — it's choosing to move forward with God anyway.

———————— † ————————

6. Fear (of the Unknown)

"When I am afraid, I put my trust in you." - *Psalm 56:3 (NIV)*
"So do not fear, for I am with you; do not be dismayed, for I am
your God. I will strengthen you and help you; I will uphold you with
my righteous right hand." - *Isaiah 41:10 (NIV)*
"Have I not commanded you? Be strong and courageous. Do not be
afraid; do not be discouraged, for the Lord your God will be with you
wherever you go." - *Joshua 1:9 (NIV)*

———————————— † ————————————

Fear has a way of creeping in when the road ahead disappears into
fog. It's that quiet whisper that says, *What if?*
*What if this doesn't work out? What if I make the wrong choice? What if I lose
everything?*

We don't like not knowing — not seeing what's next — because
uncertainty feels like being suspended between faith and freefall.

The thing most people enjoy about roller coasters is that sense of fear
about what's around the next corner or just over that rise. You know
something's coming — a drop, a twist, a turn — but part of the thrill
is not knowing exactly when it will hit. Yet when those same
moments of uncertainty show up in real life, they don't feel thrilling
at all. They produce more stress, worry, and panic than we can handle
in the moment. What excites us in a controlled circumstance can
overwhelm us when faith is required.

But God doesn't promise us clarity; He promises us *presence*. He
doesn't say, "You'll always see where you're going." He says, "I'll be
with you when you can't."

When I think about fear of the unknown, I imagine standing at the
edge of a path at night with only a lantern. The light doesn't stretch

far ahead — just enough to see the next step. But that's all God asks of us: *Take the next step.* Trust that the same God who lit this one will light the next when you get there.

Fear feeds on the future — on the things we can't predict or control. Faith, though, lives in the present. It says, "Even here, even now, I trust You."

You don't need to see the whole plan to know you're in God's hands.

———————— † ————————

Takeaway

Faith doesn't erase fear — it redirects it. Instead of asking, *"What if?"* start saying, *"Even if."*

Question for Reflection

Where in your life are you waiting for full clarity before stepping forward? What would it look like to trust God for just the next step instead?

———————— † ————————

Prayer

Lord, I admit that the unknown scares me. I want to see what's ahead, but You've asked me to walk by faith, not by sight. Help me to trust You with the steps I can't see and the outcomes I can't control. Remind me that You are already in my tomorrow, preparing the way before me. When the road ahead fades into fog, teach me to keep walking by the light You've already provided. Amen.

———————— † ————————

7. Fear (Anxiety and Overthinking)

"You will keep in perfect peace those whose minds are steadfast, because they trust in you." - *Isaiah 26:3 (NIV)*

"Do not be anxious about anything, but in every situation, by prayer and petition, with thanksgiving, present your requests to God. And the peace of God, which transcends all understanding, will guard your hearts and your minds in Christ Jesus." - *Philippians 4:6-7 (NIV)*

"Cast all your anxiety on him because he cares for you." - *1 Peter 5:7 (NIV)*

———————————— † ————————————

Sometimes fear doesn't roar — it whispers.

It shows up in the middle of the night as racing thoughts, questions with no answers, and worries that loop endlessly in your mind. You replay conversations, decisions, and outcomes like a movie that won't stop. You imagine every possible scenario — not because you don't trust God, but because you're trying to prepare for what might come next.

Fear rooted in anxiety or overthinking is really fear of losing control. For many of us, control became a kind of safety net. In my own life, too many times during childhood, other people were in charge of my world — and it didn't always turn out well for me. So I developed control issues. My logic was simple: *If I plan everything myself, I can make sure nothing bad happens to me.*

But that kind of control isn't peace — it's a prison. The tighter we grip our plans, the tighter fear grips us. Overthinking creates the illusion of control, but all it really does is exhaust the mind and drain the spirit. Fear disguises itself as responsibility, convincing us that if we can just think a little harder, plan a little better, or anticipate every possible outcome, we'll finally feel safe. But peace doesn't come from knowing — it comes from trusting.

When we overthink, we crowd God out of the conversation. We start playing both planner and protector, forgetting that only one of those roles belongs to us. Philippians 4 reminds us that true peace isn't logical — it *"transcends all understanding."* That means it comes when we stop trying to reason our way to rest and simply hand it all to Him.

Sometimes the loudest battle we'll ever fight is the one in our own minds. Fear turns our thoughts into storms, and before long, we can't tell where the waves end and our faith begins. That's when we have to remind ourselves: God is not just present in the calm — He's present in the chaos too.

You don't have to think your way out of fear.
You can pray your way through it.

———————— † ————————

Takeaway

Overthinking won't bring peace — only surrender will. When your thoughts start spinning, anchor them in the truth of who God is, not what you fear might happen.

Question for Reflection

What situations make you feel the need to control every detail — and how can you begin surrendering those to God's care today?

———————— † ————————

Prayer

Lord, I've spent so much energy trying to control what only You can. My mind races, my thoughts spiral, and peace feels just out of reach. Help me release my need to manage the unknown and trust that You are already there. Quiet the noise in my mind and calm the storm in my heart. Teach me to rest in Your perfect peace and to trade control for confidence in You. Amen.

———————————— † ————————————

8. Fear (of Failure or Inadequacy)

"My grace is sufficient for you, for my power is made perfect in weakness." - *2 Corinthians 12:9 (NIV)*
"Being confident of this, that he who began a good work in you will carry it on to completion until the day of Christ Jesus." - *Philippians 1:6 (NIV)*
"Commit to the Lord whatever you do, and he will establish your plans." - *Proverbs 16:3 (NIV)*

———————— † ————————

Failure has a way of whispering lies that sound a lot like truth. It tells you that you're not good enough, not capable enough, not spiritual enough — that somehow, you've fallen short of what God expects. Those quiet lies can shape how you see yourself and what you believe you're capable of becoming.

Fear of failure often hides beneath perfectionism. It says, *"If I just do everything right, no one will see how afraid I really am."* But that isn't freedom — it's pressure. God never asked us to be flawless; He asked us to be faithful.

When I think about fear of failure, I picture Thomas Edison and his many attempts to create the lightbulb. History says he didn't fail a thousand times — he simply discovered a thousand ways *not* to make a lightbulb. Every misstep became part of his progress. In the same way, our "failures" aren't proof of inadequacy — they're evidence of persistence, growth, and learning. They're the rough drafts that God refines into purpose.

The truth is, fear of inadequacy isn't really about failing — it's about what we believe failure says about *us*. It's the fear that maybe, deep down, we're not enough. But God never measures our worth by our performance. His love isn't dependent on our success — it's steady, constant, and undeserved.

Paul reminds us in 2 Corinthians 12:9 that God's power is made perfect in weakness. That means our shortcomings don't disqualify us; they invite His strength to take over. And Philippians 1:6 promises that He *will finish what He started* in us. Even when we stumble, He's still writing the story.

Sometimes we have to fall to remember that grace still holds. His power shines brightest where our strength runs out. Even in our mistakes, we are still His — loved, chosen, and being perfected in His timing.

If you've been afraid to take a step because you might fall, remember this: God doesn't call the qualified — He qualifies the called.

———————————— † ————————————

Takeaway

Failure doesn't define you — faith does. God's grace fills every gap where your strength ends.

Question for Reflection

Where have you allowed fear of failure or inadequacy to hold you back from what God has called you to do?

———————————— † ————————————

Prayer

Lord, You know how often I let fear of failure keep me from stepping forward. I worry about not being enough, not doing enough, not becoming enough. But Your Word reminds me that Your grace is enough. Help me rest in that truth. Teach me to see failure not as a wall but as a doorway to growth, trust, and deeper dependence on You. Remind me that You will finish the good work You began in me. Amen.

—————————— † ——————————

9. Fear (of Failing God)

"For the Lord your God is gracious and compassionate. He will not turn his face from you if you return to him." - *2 Chronicles 30:9 (NIV)*
"The Lord is compassionate and gracious, slow to anger, abounding in love." - *Psalm 103:8 (NIV)*
"There is no fear in love. But perfect love drives out fear, because fear has to do with punishment." - *1 John 4:18 (NIV)*

—————————— † ——————————

There's a kind of fear that cuts deeper than the fear of failure itself — the fear of failing *God*.
It's the quiet voice that whispers, *What if I disappoint Him? What if I've messed up one too many times? What if He's tired of me getting it wrong?*

That fear rarely comes from rebellion. It comes from *love* — from wanting so badly to please God that we start to measure our worth by our performance instead of His grace. We try to *earn* what was already given freely. And when we stumble, shame quickly follows, telling us we've somehow fallen out of His favor.

Shortly after being rescued and beginning my relationship with God, I experienced what I call my *"Hem of His Garment"* moment. I had felt the closeness of His presence so strongly — and then, suddenly, it seemed like He was gone. I grieved that silence. I thought maybe I had disappointed Him, that I'd somehow failed God. But He wasn't gone at all. He was quietly testing my sincerity, my faith, my commitment. He needed to know I was *all in* — through the good and the bad, through the presence and the silence.

God's love isn't fragile. It doesn't shatter when we fall. It doesn't withdraw when we struggle. His grace isn't earned through perfection; it's proven through persistence — through coming back again and again, even when we feel unworthy to do so.

Think about Peter. He walked with Jesus, spoke with Him, even swore loyalty to Him. Yet in one of his weakest moments, Peter denied ever knowing Him. Still, when the resurrected Christ met Peter again, He didn't condemn him — He *restored* him. God doesn't use our failures to shame us; He uses them to draw us closer.

Fear of failing God often hides under the weight of love — but true love casts out fear (1 John 4:18). When your heart's desire is to honor Him, He already knows it. What He wants isn't flawless performance; it's faithful surrender.

He knows your heart. He knows your humanity. And He already factored your failures into His plan long before you made them.

—————————— † ——————————

Takeaway

You cannot fail a God who already knew your weaknesses and chose you anyway. His grace didn't stop where your mistakes began.

Question for Reflection

Where have you been holding yourself to a standard of perfection instead of resting in God's grace?

—————————— † ——————————

Prayer

Lord, You know how deeply I want to honor You — and how much it hurts when I fall short. Remind me that Your love isn't fragile and that I can never disappoint You beyond Your mercy. When I stumble, draw me back to You — not in shame but in grace. Teach me to serve You from love, not fear, and to rest in the truth that I can never fall beyond Your reach. Amen.

———————— † ————————

When You're Wrestling with Anger

Anger is one of the most honest emotions we have — and one of the hardest to handle well. It rises fast, speaks loud, and often leaves scars on both sides. Sometimes it's aimed at others, sometimes at ourselves, and sometimes, even at God.

But anger in itself isn't sin — it's what we do with it that matters. Scripture reminds us to be "slow to anger," not because God expects us to suppress it, but because He wants to transform it. In His hands, even anger can become a tool for healing — revealing where wounds still ache and where forgiveness still needs to grow.

These devotions explore the many faces of anger — outward, inward, and upward — and the freedom that comes when we hand every burning ember over to God. Because peace isn't found in pretending we're not angry; it's found in letting Him redeem what that anger tried to destroy.

————————————— † —————————————

10. Anger (Toward Others)

"My dear brothers and sisters, take note of this: Everyone should be quick to listen, slow to speak and slow to become angry, because human anger does not produce the righteousness that God desires." - *James 1:19–20 (NIV)*

"In your anger do not sin: Do not let the sun go down while you are still angry." - *Ephesians 4:26 (NIV)*

"Refrain from anger and turn from wrath; do not fret—it leads only to evil." - *Psalm 37:8 (NIV)*

—————————— † ——————————

Anger is one of the most human emotions we experience — and one of the hardest to control. It burns fast, speaks loud, and often leaves a trail behind it. When someone wounds us with words, betrays our trust, or crosses a line, the natural instinct is to rise up and defend ourselves.

But God calls us to something higher — not suppression, but surrender.
Forgiveness is often the hardest act of faith when anger feels justified.

There's a difference between righteous anger and reactive anger. Righteous anger defends truth and justice; reactive anger defends pride and ego. The first invites God into the response; the second pushes Him out of it. And as James 1:20 reminds us, "Human anger does not produce the righteousness that God desires." It doesn't bring healing — it brings separation, from peace, from grace, and often from God Himself.

When I think about anger toward others, I picture a spark in dry grass. One careless response, one sharp word, one grudge held too long — and suddenly, what started as a spark becomes a wildfire. And like a wildfire, anger doesn't just consume others; it consumes you.

Psalm 37:8 reminds us, "Refrain from anger and turn from wrath; do not fret—it leads only to evil." Anger left unchecked doesn't solve injustice — it multiplies it. Scripture doesn't say we can't feel anger; it says, "In your anger, do not sin." That means anger itself isn't the problem; it's what we do with it. We can either hand it to God and let Him redeem it, or hold onto it and let it rot our peace.

Sometimes the people who hurt us will never apologize. Sometimes they'll never see what they did wrong. But when we keep replaying the offense, we're giving them space in our hearts that belongs to God. Letting go of anger isn't saying, "You were right." It's saying, "You no longer get to control my spirit."

————————— † —————————

Takeaway

You can't heal while holding onto hate. Anger loses its power when placed in God's hands instead of your own.

Question for Reflection

Who or what has stirred anger in your heart lately? What might it look like to hand that emotion to God instead of feeding it?

————————— † —————————

Prayer

Lord, You know my heart — the hurt, the frustration, the moments I want to defend myself instead of surrendering it to You. Teach me to be slow to anger and quick to listen. When I'm wronged, help me respond with grace instead of bitterness. Replace my frustration with Your peace and my resentment with compassion. Heal the places in me that anger has hardened, and remind me that vengeance belongs to You, not me. Amen.

———————————— † ————————————

11. Anger (Toward Yourself)

"The Lord is compassionate and gracious, slow to anger, abounding in love." - *Psalm 103:8 (NIV)*
"Therefore, there is now no condemnation for those who are in Christ Jesus." - *Romans 8:1 (NIV)*

———————————— † ————————————

Anger toward others is often loud — but anger toward ourselves can be quiet, hidden, and relentless. It shows up in self-blame, shame, and the voice that says, "You should've known better." We replay our mistakes, our missed opportunities, and our moments of weakness until they harden into self-condemnation.

For some, that anger is rooted in guilt — wishing we could undo the past. For others, it's born out of perfectionism — expecting ourselves to never fail. But both lead to the same prison: believing we must punish ourselves for what God has already forgiven.

God never asked us to be flawless. He asked us to be faithful. Yet we often hold ourselves to a standard that even He doesn't demand. Romans 8:1 reminds us that "there is now no condemnation for those who are in Christ Jesus." If God Himself has released you from judgment, why keep yourself chained to it?

When I think about self-directed anger, I picture a person trying to pick cactus leaves barehanded when there's a perfectly safe pair of gloves sitting right beside them. Every time they reach for the cactus without protection, the spines dig deeper, leaving fresh wounds where old ones haven't healed. God's grace is those gloves — freely offered, strong enough to protect, but useless if we refuse to put them on. The pain we carry isn't from the cactus alone; it's from insisting on handling it without His help.

Putting on the gloves means choosing grace — again and again — until handling your past doesn't hurt anymore.

Psalm 103:8 reminds us that the Lord is "compassionate and gracious, slow to anger, abounding in love." If that's how God treats us, shouldn't we learn to treat ourselves the same way?

Forgiving yourself doesn't mean excusing mistakes; it means accepting grace. It means choosing to believe that Jesus' sacrifice covered all sin — even the ones you still hold against yourself.

———————————— † ————————————

Takeaway

You can't heal while holding yourself hostage. Release the anger you've aimed inward and allow God's grace to fill the space where condemnation once lived.

Question for Reflection

What past mistake or moment of disappointment are you still holding against yourself — and what would it look like to see it through God's eyes instead of your own?

———————————— † ————————————

Prayer

Lord, I've been my own harshest critic. I've replayed my failures, punished myself for my flaws, and struggled to believe I deserve grace. Help me to let go of the anger I've turned inward and to receive the compassion You freely offer. Teach me to see myself the way You do — forgiven, loved, and whole. Replace my self-condemnation with peace, and remind me that Your mercy is bigger than my mistakes. Amen.

———————————— † ————————————

12. Anger (Toward God)

"The Lord is close to the brokenhearted and saves those who are crushed in spirit." - *Psalm 34:18 (NIV)*
"Trust in the Lord with all your heart and lean not on your own understanding." - *Proverbs 3:5 (NIV)*
"For our struggle is not against flesh and blood, but against the rulers, against the authorities, against the powers of this dark world and against the spiritual forces of evil in the heavenly realms." - *Ephesians 6:12 (NIV)*

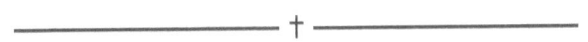

Anger toward God can be one of the hardest kinds of anger to admit. It hides behind phrases like, "I'm fine," or "I've forgiven," but deep down there's hurt — disappointment, confusion, maybe even betrayal. We know in our heads that God is good, but our hearts struggle to reconcile that truth when life shatters around us.

What separated me from God as a teenager was my belief that He didn't care about me — that He allowed my father to abuse me. I carried such anger at God for not being there, for not protecting me. I thought He had turned away when I needed Him most. But years later, after being rescued and returning to His flock, I finally saw the truth: He was there. Every moment. He never left me. And He certainly didn't have a hand in what my father did.

We're so quick to blame God when things don't go as we want or expect them to. But why are we so quick to blame Him and not the enemy? It's not God's actions causing our pain and misery — it's the enemy's deception. The devil thrives on confusion, twisting our pain into lies about God's character. He whispers, "See? God didn't stop it. He doesn't care about you." But that's not truth — that's warfare.

Ephesians 6:12 reminds us that our struggle isn't against flesh and blood — and it's not against God either. It's against the spiritual forces of evil that want nothing more than to pull us away from Him. The enemy knows that if he can get us angry at God, he can keep us from God.

God isn't the author of our pain; He's the healer of it. When we bring Him our anger, our accusations, even our tears — He doesn't flinch. He listens. He holds. He restores. Psalm 34:18 says He is "close to the brokenhearted and saves those who are crushed in spirit." He isn't offended by your honesty; He's moved by it.

When I finally handed my anger to God, I didn't find punishment — I found peace.

Anger toward God doesn't disqualify you from His love — it's often the doorway back into His arms.

———————— † ————————

Takeaway

God isn't afraid of your anger — He wants your honesty. The same God you question is the God who will heal what hurt you.

Question for Reflection

Have you ever been angry at God for something painful in your life? What might happen if you invited Him into that anger instead of shutting Him out?

———————— † ————————

Prayer

Lord, I've been angry with You — hurt, confused, and questioning why things happened the way they did. I've blamed You for pain You never caused and turned away from the comfort You offered. But today, I release that anger. I forgive You, Lord — not because You were ever wrong, but because I need to let go of the hurt I tied to Your name. I know now that You were always there — protecting, guiding, and loving me through the storm. Forgive me for misplacing my anger, and heal the places in me that still ache. Remind me that my pain was never Your plan, but the enemy's attack. Thank You for never leaving me, even when I pushed You away. I love You, Lord — and I trust You again. Amen.

———————— † ————————

When Others Let You Down

Sometimes, the deepest wounds don't come from strangers — they come from the people we trusted most. Friends who turned away. Family who didn't show up. Fellow believers who spoke in judgment instead of love.

It's easy to love when life feels safe. It's much harder when love has left bruises on your heart. But healing requires us to face the pain, not bury it. God never promised that people wouldn't fail us — He promised that *He* never would.

When others let us down, the temptation is to close off, to build walls, to stop believing that anyone is safe. Yet, even in betrayal and disappointment, God whispers, *"You can trust Me. I can handle your hurt."*

This section is for the moments when forgiveness feels impossible, when trust feels broken beyond repair, and when your heart aches to believe that love — real love — can still exist after heartbreak.

Because while people may fail you, God never will. And when you let Him, He can turn even your deepest wound into a doorway for deeper grace.

———————————— † ————————————

13. Offense

"Cast all your anxiety on Him because He cares for you." - *1 Peter 5:7 (NIV)*
"A person's wisdom yields patience; it is to one's glory to overlook an offense." - *Proverbs 19:11 (NIV)*
"Bear with each other and forgive one another if any of you has a grievance against someone. Forgive as the Lord forgave you." - *Colossians 3:13 (NIV)*

Offense is one of the heaviest burdens we can carry — mostly because we're the ones who choose to carry it.

I look at offense and hurt like this: every time someone wounds or offends me, they hand me a potato-sized rock that I take and hold onto. Hurt after hurt, rock after rock, until—finally—I'm weighed down with a ton of them, straining under the pressure. But here's the truth: I'm the only one carrying them. The people who hurt me have long since wandered off, weightless in the wake of their actions.

At no point did anyone ever say I had to keep holding onto those rocks. I don't! I can let them go. I can walk up to the feet of Jesus and drop every single one there for Him to deal with.

But letting go of offense doesn't always happen in one big dump of rocks. Sometimes it's one stone at a time — one moment, one wound, one person. Some of those rocks have names. Some carry years of history. But none of them were meant for your hands.

Proverbs 19:11 says, "It is to one's glory to overlook an offense." That doesn't mean pretending you weren't hurt — it means choosing healing over bitterness. When you release an offense to God, you're not excusing what happened; you're refusing to let it keep ruling your heart.

Offense is sneaky. It disguises itself as self-protection, convincing us that holding onto the pain keeps us safe from being hurt again. But all it really does is harden our hearts and isolate us from peace.

Jesus carried a cross for the very people who offended Him — mocked Him, betrayed Him, and nailed Him to it. If He could forgive from that place, surely we can begin to forgive from ours.

When we drop our rocks at His feet, He doesn't hand them back. He builds something better with them — strength, compassion, empathy, and grace.

———————— † ————————

Takeaway

You don't have to carry offense. You are free to release it. Jesus cares for you, and His shoulders are strong enough for every rock you've been holding.

Question for Reflection

What "rocks" are you still carrying today — and what would it look like to lay them down, one by one, at Jesus' feet?

———————— † ————————

Prayer

Lord, I don't want to carry offense any longer. Help me recognize when I'm holding onto hurts and remind me that I can bring them to You. Teach me to walk lighter, freer, and closer to You each day. Where there was bitterness, grow compassion. Where there was pain, bring peace. And when I'm tempted to pick up those rocks again, gently remind me that You've already carried them for me.

Amen.

———————— † ————————

14. Betrayal (Personal)

"Even my close friend, someone I trusted, one who shared my bread, has turned against me." - *Psalm 41:9 (NIV)*

"After He had said this, Jesus was troubled in spirit and testified, 'Very truly I tell you, one of you is going to betray me.'" - *John 13:21 (NIV)*

"The Lord will fight for you; you need only to be still." - *Exodus 14:14 (NIV)*

"The Lord is my strength and my shield; my heart trusts in Him, and He helps me." - *Psalm 28:7 (NIV)*

——————————— † ———————————

There's no pain quite like betrayal. It cuts deeper because it doesn't come from enemies — it comes from those you trusted most. The friend who turned their back, the loved one who broke your heart, the confidant who used your vulnerability against you. Betrayal doesn't just bruise the heart; it shakes the soul.

When trust is shattered, your heart questions everything: "How could they do this to me? Did I mean anything to them? How do I ever trust again?" Those questions echo in the spaces where connection once lived. And it's in those same spaces that bitterness, anger, and disbelief try to take root.

Jesus knew betrayal firsthand — not in theory, but in the rawest, most personal way possible. Judas wasn't a stranger; he was one of the twelve, one who walked beside Him, saw the miracles, and shared His table. John 13:21 tells us that "Jesus was troubled in spirit" when He revealed that one of His own was about to betray Him. Imagine that moment — the heaviness in His heart, the sting of knowing that someone He had poured love, teaching, and trust into would trade it all away for silver. Jesus didn't just know betrayal; He felt it. Yet still, He chose forgiveness. Still, He chose the cross.

That moment reveals something powerful — that betrayal says more about the betrayer's heart than the betrayed one's worth.

When I think about personal betrayal, I imagine a knife — whether intentional or not — plunged into my back to wound and hurt me. Yet when I surrender that wound to God, that same blade becomes the tool He uses to carve something new and beautiful in my heart. It's not that He caused the wound — but He refuses to let it be wasted. The hurt that once bled resentment can, through His hands, become a scar of wisdom, empathy, and strength.

Exodus 14:14 reminds us, "The Lord will fight for you; you need only to be still." You don't have to avenge the wrong or prove your innocence. God sees. God knows. And in His timing, He brings both justice and healing.

Betrayal may change how you see people, but it doesn't have to change how you see God. He is still trustworthy. He is still faithful. He is still the One who binds up the brokenhearted and restores everything the enemy tried to steal.

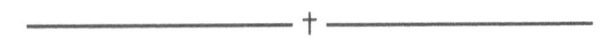

Takeaway

Betrayal may break your trust in people, but it doesn't have to break your faith in God. The same God who saw the betrayal will also be the One who heals the wound it left behind.

Question for Reflection

Who or what comes to mind when you think of betrayal? How can you begin to release that pain and invite God to restore trust — not just in others, but in your own heart?

———————— † ————————

Prayer

Lord, betrayal hurts in ways words can't explain. I've been broken by people I trusted and disappointed by those I loved. But I know You understand — You were betrayed too. You felt the sting of being turned against by someone close to You, and yet You still chose love. Help me lay down the need to make sense of it all, and instead, let You fight for me. Heal the places in my heart that still bleed from broken trust. Teach me to forgive, not to forget, but to be free. Help me to trust again — first in You, and in time, with others. Turn this wound into wisdom and let it point me back to Your faithfulness. Amen.

———————— † ————————

15. Betrayal (Spiritual / Church Hurt)

"The Lord is near to all who call on Him, to all who call on Him in truth." - *Psalm 145:18 (NIV)*
"Even my close friend, someone I trusted, one who shared my bread, has turned against me." - *Psalm 41:9 (NIV)*
"But Jesus said, 'Father, forgive them, for they do not know what they are doing.'" - *Luke 23:34 (NIV)*

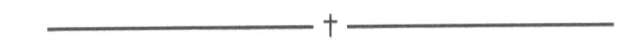

There's a unique kind of pain that comes when the very people who were meant to represent God end up wounding you instead. It's one thing to be hurt by the world — but another entirely to be hurt by the church. Spiritual betrayal cuts deep because it confuses the heart. We expect the church to be a refuge, a place of healing and safety, but sometimes we find judgment, gossip, rejection, or hypocrisy instead.

It's in those moments that trust begins to crack — not just trust in people, but sometimes trust in God Himself. We think, "If these are His people, how could they do this to me?" And that's exactly where the enemy loves to step in — whispering that God Himself must not care. But that's a lie.

God never asked us to put our faith in people; He asked us to put our faith in Him. People will always be imperfect — even those in leadership, even those who mean well. Jesus experienced betrayal too — not just from strangers, but from one of His own disciples, someone who walked beside Him, learned from Him, and shared His table. He understands your pain intimately. And like Jesus, Paul also faced deep wounds within the church — rejected, questioned, and criticized by those he was called to love.

When you've been wounded by the church, it's tempting to walk away from both the building and the Body. But don't confuse people's failures with God's character. The church may have failed you, but Jesus never did.

Even Paul knew what it was like to be hurt by the very believers he was called to shepherd. In his letters to the Church in Corinth, he poured out both love and correction. They questioned his authority, rejected his message, and spoke harshly against him — yet Paul didn't turn away. He didn't respond with bitterness or pride. Instead, he continued to teach, encourage, and forgive. His faithfulness to God wasn't dependent on people's treatment of him — it was rooted in God's calling on his life.

The Corinthian church reminds us that even God's people can act in ways that wound — but it also reminds us that grace is still possible, and restoration can still come.

Psalm 145:18 says, "The Lord is near to all who call on Him, to all who call on Him in truth." When the pain of betrayal makes you feel distant from God, know that He's still near — closer than the hurt, stronger than the wound, and gentler than the judgment you've endured.

Takeaway

People may fail you in the name of God, but God Himself never will. Healing begins when you stop confusing the actions of the broken with the heart of the Healer.

Question for Reflection

Have you ever confused the failure of people with the faithfulness of God? What might it look like to separate the two and begin healing with Him again?

Prayer

Lord, You know the pain of being betrayed by those who claimed to stand for You. You know the ache of being misunderstood, rejected, or hurt by people who were supposed to love like You do. Help me separate who You are from what was done to me. Heal the wounds caused in Your name, and remind me that You never left my side. Teach me to forgive — not to excuse the wrong, but to free my heart from the weight it's carried for too long. Like Paul, help me love people through the pain and continue walking in my calling, trusting that You're still building Your church — even through broken vessels. Amen.

16. Projection (When You're the Target)

"Do not repay evil with evil or insult with insult. On the contrary, repay evil with blessing, because to this you were called so that you may inherit a blessing." - *1 Peter 3:9 (NIV)*

"The Lord will fight for you; you need only to be still." - *Exodus 14:14 (NIV)*

"Blessed are you when people insult you, persecute you and falsely say all kinds of evil against you because of Me." - *Matthew 5:11 (NIV)*

———————————— † ————————————

One of the hardest lessons I've had to learn is that people don't always see you for who you are — they see you through the lens of their own pain.

Projection happens when someone takes their own insecurities, guilt, or shame and places them on someone else. It's a defense mechanism — and if you're the target, it can hurt deeply. You find yourself wondering what you did wrong, when in truth, their reaction isn't about you at all. It's about something in them they haven't yet healed.

You've probably heard the saying, *"Hurt people hurt people."* And it's true. When someone is hurting, they often want others to feel that same pain. Misery craves company. So they lash out, gossip, criticize, or project — hoping, maybe even subconsciously, that if others feel as low as they do, their own pain will sting a little less.

But that's not healing — that's spreading infection. And we can't fix someone else's wounds by bleeding with them.

I've been there — misunderstood, accused, blamed for things I didn't do. I used to take it personally. I'd try to explain myself, defend myself, or fix whatever someone was feeling toward me. But the more I tried to control how others saw me, the more I lost sight of how God sees me.

The truth is, you can't control other people's projections — but you can control your response.

1 Peter 3:9 tells us not to repay evil with evil, but to respond with blessing. That's not weakness; that's spiritual maturity. It's choosing to trust God to handle what your heart can't.

When I think about being the target of projection, I picture standing in front of a mirror someone else is holding. The reflection is warped and distorted — not because of who you are, but because of the cracks in their glass. The reflection they show you doesn't define you; it reveals them.

That's where Exodus 14:14 speaks the loudest: "The Lord will fight for you; you need only to be still." Sometimes the best defense is quiet confidence in who God says you are.

Even Jesus endured projection. In Matthew 5:11, He said, "Blessed are you when people insult you and falsely say all kinds of evil against you because of Me." People projected their fear, guilt, and anger onto Him — yet He responded with compassion, forgiveness, and truth.

So when you find yourself on the receiving end of someone's brokenness, remember: you are not what they say you are. You are who God says you are.

Takeaway:
When others project their pain onto you, don't absorb it — reflect God's peace instead. Their projection doesn't define you; it reveals where they still need healing.

Question for Reflection:
Are you carrying pain that someone else projected onto you? How would your heart change if you handed that pain to God instead of holding onto it?

—————————— † ——————————

Prayer:

Lord, help me see others through compassion, even when they misunderstand or mistreat me. Remind me that hurt people hurt people — and that I don't have to respond in kind. When I'm the target of someone's pain, let me be a reflection of Your peace, not a mirror of their hurt. You are my defender and my refuge.

Amen.

—————————— † ——————————

When Doubt Creeps In

Even the strongest believers face moments when faith feels like a flickering flame.
You pray, but the silence stretches longer than your patience. You trust, but the outcome doesn't make sense. You believe, but still — you wonder.

Doubt doesn't always mean disbelief; sometimes it's just a tired heart asking honest questions. It sneaks in quietly after disappointment, betrayal, or loss, whispering, *"What if God forgot me?"* or *"What if I'm not enough for what He's called me to do?"*

But even when your faith feels fragile, God's faithfulness is not.
He doesn't shame your uncertainty — He steps into it. He doesn't abandon you in your questions — He meets you there.

This section is for the moments when your belief wavers, when the path feels unclear, and when your trust in yourself — or even in God — starts to shake. Because the truth is, your faith isn't measured by the size of your confidence, but by the direction of your reach.

Keep reaching toward Him, even when your grip feels weak.
He'll hold on for the both of you.

———————— † ————————

17. Doubt (In Yourself & Your Calling)

"Trust in the Lord with all your heart and lean not on your own understanding; in all your ways submit to Him, and He will make your paths straight." - *Proverbs 3:5–6 (NIV)*

"...Lord, I believe; help my unbelief." - *Mark 9:24 (NKJV)*

"Being confident of this, that He who began a good work in you will carry it on to completion until the day of Christ Jesus." - *Philippians 1:6 (NIV)*

———————————— † ————————————

Sometimes doubt doesn't sound like rebellion — it sounds like exhaustion. It's not that you've stopped believing in God; it's that you've started struggling to believe in yourself.

This semester, I've found myself buried under the weight of uncertainty — doors that didn't open, opportunities that fell through, and silence that feels a little too long. I thought I'd be in practicum by now, but every path I pursued seemed to end with another "not yet." Now, with another deadline looming, I can feel doubt creeping in: *Am I really meant to do this? Did I misunderstand God's calling? Am I even capable of getting where He's leading me?*

When I think about this kind of doubt, I picture a traveler standing in thick fog. The path is still there — they just can't see it right now. Each step forward feels risky, uncertain, and lonely. But the Guide hasn't left. He's simply walking one step ahead, asking them to trust His voice more than their vision.

Proverbs 3:5–6 tells us to "trust in the Lord with all your heart and lean not on your own understanding." When we can't see clearly, He doesn't ask us to map it out — He just asks us to keep walking in obedience. Doubt tells you that your uncertainty disqualifies you. Faith says that it's proof you're still in the process.

Mark 9:24 captures that tension perfectly: "Lord, I believe; help my unbelief." That prayer has carried me through more seasons than I can count. It's the reminder that God doesn't shame our doubt — He meets us in it.

And Philippians 1:6 whispers hope to the weary heart: "He who began a good work in you will carry it on to completion." The same God who called you to this journey hasn't changed His mind. Delays aren't denials — they're often divine pauses, giving your roots time to grow deeper before your calling grows wider.

Maybe the victory isn't in having all the answers, but in simply showing up — believing that God's still writing this chapter, even when you can't see how it ends.

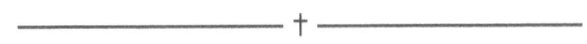

Takeaway

Doubt doesn't mean you've lost your faith — it means you're still fighting for it. Keep moving, even when you can't see the finish line. God's hand hasn't left your story.

Question for Reflection

What part of your calling feels clouded by doubt right now? What truth do you need to remind yourself of to keep taking the next step?

Prayer

Lord, I'm tired of wondering if I'm still on the right path. The waiting has worn me down, and the silence feels heavy. But even here — in the doubt and the in-between — I choose to trust You. Remind me that my uncertainty doesn't cancel Your calling; it deepens my dependence on You. Help me walk by faith when I can't see the way forward, resting in the promise that You always finish what You start. Amen.

———————————— † ————————————

18. Doubt (in God)

"In you, Lord my God, I put my trust." - *Psalm 25:1 (NIV)*
"Immediately the boy's father exclaimed, 'I do believe; help me overcome my unbelief!'" - *Mark 9:24 (NIV)*
"The thief comes only to steal and kill and destroy; I have come that they may have life, and have it to the full." - *John 10:10 (NIV)*

———————— † ————————

The enemy's greatest weapon isn't fear or temptation — it's doubt in God.

The enemy knows he doesn't stand a chance when we're walking in faith — when our hearts are full of trust, joy, and confidence in who God is. But when things get tough — when the spiritual battles rage, when pain takes hold, when prayers seem to go unanswered — that's when he starts whispering his favorite lie: *"You can't really trust God, can you?"*

Doubt is the enemy's foothold — and he wields it masterfully.

As children, he whispers through our pain:
"If God is real, why did He let this happen?"
"Why didn't He stop it?"

That's what separated me from God when I was young. I couldn't reconcile a loving, caring, powerful God with the reality of the abuse and suffering I endured. My heart cried out, *"How can God be real if He allows such evil to touch the innocent?"*

And for years, that doubt built a wall between us.

But as adults, the enemy changes tactics. The questions evolve as we grow older, but the goal remains the same — to separate us from God.

"Why would God let me lose my loved one?"
"Why didn't He save my job, my home, my family?"
"Why hasn't He sent someone to love me?"

Each unanswered question is a chisel, carving away at our faith — unless we learn to see doubt for what it really is: a spiritual attack.

Even in our final days, the enemy doesn't stop. He preys on our pain, our exhaustion, our fear of the unknown:
"Why won't God just let me die already?"
"Why am I suffering like this?"

The enemy's goal has always been the same since the Garden of Eden, to make us question God's goodness, His timing, and His love.

But doubt, when surrendered back into God's hands, can become the very soil where deeper faith takes root and flourishes.

Mark 9:24 tells of a desperate father crying out to Jesus, "I do believe; help me overcome my unbelief!" That moment shows us something beautiful: God doesn't condemn our doubt — He meets us in it.

And for me, that's where Psalm 25:1 comes in.

"In you, Lord my God, I put my trust."

That's my anchor in the chaos tornadoes of life. When everything is spinning, when the enemy's voice grows loud, that verse pulls me back to center, back to truth, back to Him.

Faith isn't the absence of doubt. It's choosing to keep walking even while doubt tries to slow you down.

When you feel that whisper — *"How could God let this happen?"* — remember: that's not God's voice. That's the enemy, trying to separate you from the very One who's holding you together.

So when doubt creeps in, speak truth louder than the lie. When you don't understand, lean in closer to the One who does. And when you can't find the words to pray, whisper like that father struggling with doubt did: *"Lord, I believe — help my unbelief."*

Even your weakest faith is stronger than the enemy's loudest lie when it's anchored in Jesus.

———————— † ————————

Takeaway

Doubt is the enemy's weapon, but it doesn't have to be your downfall. Anchor your heart in God's truth, and He'll turn your questions into closeness and your fear into faith.

Question for Reflection

When doubt starts whispering in your ear, what promise of God can you anchor yourself to instead?

———————— † ————————

Prayer

Lord, You know my heart — every doubt, every question, every fear. The enemy tries to use them to pull me away, but I choose to run toward You instead. Anchor me in Your Word and Your truth. When I struggle to believe, remind me that even the smallest faith is still faith — and in Your hands, it's enough. I believe, Lord — help my unbelief. Amen.

———————— † ————————

When You Struggle To Trust

Trust is one of the hardest lessons we ever learn — because it's almost always taught through pain. Broken promises, betrayal, and disappointment chip away at our confidence until we start believing that safety lies in control instead of surrender.

But true trust isn't blind — it's anchored. It doesn't come from perfect people or predictable plans; it comes from knowing the One who never changes.

Learning to trust again begins with placing our hearts back in God's hands. When we trust Him, we slowly find the courage to trust others — and eventually, to trust ourselves again.

These devotions explore what it looks like to trust when life doesn't make sense, when people let you down, and when you doubt your own judgment. Because the truth is, trust isn't about never falling — it's about knowing who will catch you when you do.

———————— † ————————

19. Trusting God (When His Plan Doesn't Make Sense)

"Trust in the Lord with all your heart and lean not on your own understanding; in all your ways submit to Him, and He will make your paths straight." - *Proverbs 3:5–6 (NIV)*

"Be still, and know that I am God." - *Psalm 46:10 (NIV)*

"The Lord will fight for you; you need only to be still." - *Exodus 14:14 (NIV)*

———————————— † ————————————

Trusting God sounds easy — until the waiting starts.

When I began working toward the degree I should have gotten decades ago, I had a plan. I wanted to be a forensic psychologist, to study the minds of criminals, to understand what drives the darkness. But that was before I was rescued — before God stepped in and redirected my path. Once I became His child, He shifted everything — my purpose, my direction, even my desires. He turned my heart toward becoming a mental health counselor, helping others heal instead of merely analyzing their pain.

I thought that once I followed His call, the path would smooth out. But here I am — struggling to find a practicum site, watching deadlines come and go, wondering what God is doing and if I somehow misheard Him. I know His timing is perfect, but trusting that truth while I'm stuck in this in-between is hard.

When I think about trust, I picture a puzzle missing a few key pieces. You can see the outline of what it's supposed to be, but the gaps keep it from feeling complete. That's what trusting God feels like sometimes — holding onto the picture of His promises while not yet seeing how it all fits together.

Proverbs 3:5–6 tells us to trust in the Lord with all your heart and not to lean on our own understanding. But sometimes our "understanding" is the only thing that makes sense to us because we're staring at it in the moment: the perfect plan, the incomplete checklist, the tight timeline all seem important right now. When God redirects, delays, or seems silent, His timing stretches our faith in ways comfort never could.

Psalm 46:10 says, "Be still, and know that I am God." Stillness doesn't mean doing nothing; it means surrendering everything, even that perfect plan you had for your life. It's choosing to believe that even when you can't trace His hand, you can still trust His heart.

And Exodus 14:14 reminds us, "The Lord will fight for you; you need only to be still." When Israel stood trapped between the Red Sea and an approaching army, God didn't panic — He parted the waters. Maybe your practicum delay isn't punishment; maybe it's preparation for something far greater than you imagined.

God's plan doesn't always follow our deadlines. But He's never late. The very place you feel stuck is where He's building something sacred. It's not just a location you're stuck and delayed at, but deeper calling for you to trust Him more.

Takeaway:
Trust isn't proven in answered prayers — it's forged in waiting ones. The delay doesn't mean God has forgotten; it means He's still writing the story.

Question for Reflection:
Do you feel stuck along life's path? Where is God asking you to pause your plans so He can prove His presence?

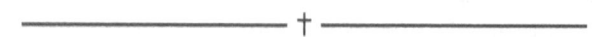

Prayer:

Lord, I admit — this waiting is hard. I want to see the plan, to understand the "why." But You've called me to trust, not to control. Help me to let go of my timeline and rest in Yours. Remind me that You haven't forgotten me, and that every closed door and missed deadline still leads exactly where You want me to be. Strengthen my faith in the waiting, and help me trust that when it's time, You'll open the right door — and I'll be ready to walk through it. Amen.

---------------- † ----------------

20. Trusting God (When His Way Replaces Yours)

"For my thoughts are not your thoughts, neither are your ways my ways," declares the Lord. - *Isaiah 55:8 (NIV)*

"Trust in the Lord with all your heart and lean not on your own understanding; in all your ways submit to Him, and He will make your paths straight." - *Proverbs 3:5–6 (NIV)*

"Many are the plans in a person's heart, but it is the Lord's purpose that prevails." - *Proverbs 19:21 (NIV)*

———————————— † ————————————

Trusting God's way over our own sounds simple, until we actually have to do it.

Before I was rescued, near the end of the pandemic, I was facing homelessness. Bills were piling up, my rent was about to nearly double, and I was barely hanging on. A friend offered to rent me a room in her house, but my pride said, "No way." I was an independent, grown adult. I was going to figure it out on my own.

Twice more, she offered. Twice more, I refused. I was determined to find something I could afford — to live my life *my* way.

Then, out of nowhere, this calm washed over me. A peace I couldn't explain settled in my chest, and I heard a still, quiet voice say, "It's going to be okay. Accept the offer."

So I did.

And that "tiny voice"? That was God.

Looking back now, I can see that He was positioning me for rescue. For healing. For a complete redirection of my life — one that would bring me closer to Him and to the people He would use to restore me.

Sometimes we don't recognize God's plan because it doesn't look like ours. His way may feel uncomfortable, humbling, or even confusing. But His plan is always better — even when it requires us to surrender the illusion of control.

Isaiah 55:8 says, "My thoughts are not your thoughts, neither are your ways my ways." We don't have to understand everything He's doing — we just have to trust that He's doing something.

When I think about trusting God's way, I picture a winding road through fog. You can only see a few feet ahead, but you keep moving because you trust the road is still there — that it will lead you where you're supposed to go. That's what faith looks like.

God's plans don't always make sense in the moment, but they're always good in the end. My path to safety didn't come through self-sufficiency — it came through surrender.

Takeaway:
Trusting God's way means giving up our need to control the outcome. It's believing His "not yet" or "not that" is part of His greater "yes."

Question for Reflection:
Where is God asking you to surrender your plan so He can reveal His?

Prayer:

Lord, You know how tightly I hold onto my own plans, how hard it is for me to let go. But time and again, You've proven that Your way is better — even when I don't understand it. Help me to trust You more fully. Quiet my pride, calm my fears, and remind me that peace always follows obedience. Thank You for guiding me, even when I didn't want to be guided. Amen.

—————————— † ——————————

21. Trust (in Others)

"It is better to take refuge in the Lord than to trust in man." - *Psalm 118:8 (NIV)*

"Trust in the Lord with all your heart and lean not on your own understanding; in all your ways submit to Him, and He will make your paths straight." - *Proverbs 3:5–6 (NIV)*

"When I am afraid, I put my trust in You." - *Psalm 56:3 (NIV)*

———————— † ————————

After we've been let down by people who were supposed to love and protect us, trust can start to feel like a gamble we no longer want to take.

When your parents, siblings, or those closest to you fail to show up in the ways you need them most, it leaves a mark. You learn early that "blood is thicker than water" isn't always true — and suddenly, trusting anyone feels risky.

That's been one of my biggest struggles too: learning to trust others when my own family taught me that even the people who are supposed to be there sometimes aren't. If my own flesh and blood couldn't be counted on, how could I expect anyone else to be?

And then, just when you muster the courage to let your guard down, you get disappointed again — another no-show, another broken promise, another reminder that trust can hurt. So you build walls to protect yourself, and you stop asking. You stop hoping. You stop trusting.

For several milestone birthdays, I tried to plan something special — a big celebration surrounded by friends and family. Each time, people eagerly said they'd come… only to cancel at the last minute.

This year, as I approached the big 5-0, I wanted to plan something grand and worthy of half a century of life! but I couldn't bring myself

to do it. The fear of disappointment was too strong.
So I scrapped the big plans and chose a small cookout instead.

And then even that started to unravel.

Old fears began to whisper: *No one wants to celebrate you. You're going to be disappointed again. No one cares about you.*

So I stopped trying to plan things for other people to show up to. Instead, I started planning moments for me and God — little adventures each month: a beach day, a mountain drive, a road trip. Just to spend intentional time with Him.

It wasn't about trusting people anymore. It was about learning to trust God — to see beauty and joy in the life He's given me, even if others don't always show up the way I'd hoped.

Because here's the truth: people will fail us sometimes — not always out of malice, but out of their own limitations. God never will.

Proverbs 3:5–6 reminds us, "Trust in the Lord with all your heart and lean not on your own understanding." Trusting Him doesn't mean closing yourself off to others; it means giving Him the right to hold your heart first, so when others let you down, you don't fall apart.

When you place your trust in God, He teaches you how to trust again — not blindly, but wisely. He helps you see the difference between people who are meant to walk with you and those who are only meant to wave as they pass by.

And when you start seeing your worth through His eyes, you realize something beautiful: you were never unworthy of love or celebration — you were simply waiting for the One who would never forget your invitation.

———————— † ————————

Takeaway:
Learning to trust again doesn't start with people — it starts with God. Once you trust Him with your heart, He'll show you who's safe to let back in.

Question for Reflection:
Who have you been hesitant to trust again — and how might God be asking you to start rebuilding that trust, one small step at a time?

———————————— † ————————————

Prayer:
Lord, You know how hard it's been for me to trust after being disappointed by people I love. Help me to trust You first — to rest in the safety of Your love and guidance. Teach me how to see others through Your eyes, to forgive, and to open my heart again when the time is right. Thank You for never letting me down, for being faithful even when others aren't. Amen.

———————————— † ————————————

When You Need Strength to Keep Going

There comes a point in every journey where the battle shifts from *breaking down* to *pressing through*. You've faced the fears, the anger, the hurt, the doubt — and you've learned what it means to trust again. But now comes the real test: the walk forward.

Because even after healing begins, life doesn't stop.
There are still long days, heavy hearts, and uphill climbs. There are moments when faith feels like work, when the fire burns low, and when it takes everything in you just to take the next step.

That's where strength — *real, God-given strength* — becomes more than a word. It becomes a lifeline.

This isn't the kind of strength that flexes or fights back; it's the kind that kneels, breathes, and whispers, *"Lord, help me take one more step."* It's the courage to keep showing up when you'd rather give up. It's the quiet power that comes from knowing you're not walking alone.

And here's the beautiful thing: God doesn't ask you to carry the weight of the world — just to keep walking in His.
He supplies the strength for today, the courage for tomorrow, and the hope that shines just beyond the horizon.

So take a breath. Lift your head. And keep going.
You've come too far to stop now — and God's not finished yet.

———————————— † ————————————

22. Courage

"Have I not commanded you? Be strong and courageous. Do not be afraid; do not be discouraged, for the Lord your God will be with you wherever you go." - *Joshua 1:9 (NIV)*

"When I am afraid, I put my trust in You." - *Psalm 56:3 (NIV)*

"The Lord is my light and my salvation—whom shall I fear?" - *Psalm 27:1 (NIV)*

Courage isn't about being fearless — it's about moving forward *despite* fear.

When God told Joshua to be strong and courageous, He wasn't ignoring the reality of Joshua's fear. Joshua was stepping into massive shoes, leading a nation into unknown territory. But God didn't say, "Don't feel afraid." He said, "Don't let fear stop you."

That's courage — obedience in motion, even when your knees are trembling.

When I think of courage, I think of the Cowardly Lion from *The Wizard of Oz*. It's easy to be brave when we've got our "growl," when we feel strong and confident. But true courage — the kind God calls us to — shows up when we feel like that lion did: scared, uncertain, and unworthy.

Real courage isn't the absence of fear; it's the determination to keep walking down the Yellow Brick Road anyway — trusting that somewhere ahead, God has already prepared the victory.

And perhaps no one embodied that better than David.

When David stood before Goliath, he wasn't a trained warrior. He didn't have armor, a sword, or an army to back him up — just a sling, a few smooth stones, and unshakable faith that God would deliver him.

Can you imagine the fear pulsing through him as he stepped into that arena? A young shepherd boy facing a towering, battle-hardened giant — a man everyone else was too terrified to confront.

But David leaned into the Lord instead of his fear. His courage didn't come from confidence in himself — it came from knowing who stood beside him.

With one small stone and complete trust, he conquered what others called impossible.

That's what courage looks like for us, too. We may not face physical giants, but we face emotional, spiritual, and situational ones — fear, rejection, failure, uncertainty. Yet, like David, we're called to pick up our stones, step forward, and trust that the same God who guided his aim will guide ours.

Psalm 56:3 says, "When I am afraid, I put my trust in You." That's not pretending fear doesn't exist — it's placing it in God's hands and saying, *"You're bigger than this."*

When I think about courage, I also picture a candle in the dark. It doesn't light up the entire room, but it burns bright enough to take the next step. Courage doesn't eliminate darkness — it simply refuses to let the darkness win.

And the most powerful truth? Courage doesn't come from within us — it comes from *Who walks beside us.* Joshua 1:9 reminds us, "The Lord your God will be with you wherever you go."

That means you're never standing in front of your Goliath alone.

———————— † ————————

Takeaway:
True courage isn't found in your "growl" — it's found in your God. Even when you're trembling, He fights beside you.

Question for Reflection:
What "giant" are you facing today? How might your courage grow if you confronted your giant like David, trusting that God's strength is greater than your fear?

———————————— † ————————————

Prayer:
Lord, thank You that courage doesn't mean I have to be fearless — it means I trust You more than my fear. When I face my giants, remind me that You are the One who fights for me. Help me to be like David — brave not because of my power, but because of Your presence. Give me courage to walk forward, even when I feel like the Cowardly Lion, trembling, yet determined to keep moving in faith because You are with me. Amen.

———————————— † ————————————

23. Strength

"…My grace is sufficient for you, for My power is made perfect in weakness." - *2 Corinthians 12:9 (NIV)*

"The Lord is my strength and my shield; my heart trusts in Him, and He helps me." - *Psalm 28:7 (NIV)*

"But those who hope in the Lord will renew their strength. They will soar on wings like eagles; they will run and not grow weary, they will walk and not be faint." - *Isaiah 40:31 (NIV)*

------------------ † ------------------

There comes a point in every journey where strength doesn't look like running anymore — it looks like still standing. Maybe even crawling. Or, sometimes, just breathing.

We often imagine strength as bold and loud — the roar of victory, the lifted victor's trophy held high. But sometimes, strength is quiet. It's the whisper that says, *"I can't, but God can."*

Tonight, I crossed a finish line I didn't think I could make it to. The work was hard, the emotions heavier, and the outcome uncertain. But I showed up anyway. Not perfectly. Not powerfully. But faithfully. And maybe that's the truest form of strength there is.

When I think about strength, I picture a long-distance runner fighting with everything they have to take those final steps across the finish line. Their body is breaking down with each stride, tears streaming down their cheeks — and yet they push on. What moves me even more is when another runner, their competitor, stops their own race to slip an arm around that exhausted runner's shoulders and help them cross the line.

That's strength too. It shows up as compassion in motion, love in action. That's what God's strength looks like in us.

2 Corinthians 12:9 reminds us that His power is made perfect in weakness. Strength isn't the absence of weakness. It's His grace in motion. It's trusting that even when you have nothing left to give, He'll carry you the rest of the way.

Psalm 28:7 says, "The Lord is my strength and my shield; my heart trusts in Him, and He helps me." Even when your energy runs out, His help doesn't.

And Isaiah 40:31 promises that those who hope in the Lord will renew their strength. Notice it doesn't say "those who never get tired." God never shames your exhaustion — He meets you in it.

Maybe tonight isn't about finishing strong but finishing faithful. And that's all God wants from you.

———————— † ————————

Takeaway:
Strength isn't always power; sometimes it's perseverance — and sometimes it's stopping to lift another weary soul beside you.

Question for Reflection:
Where do you need to let God carry you — or where might He be asking you to help carry someone else across their own finish line?

———————— † ————————

Prayer:

Lord, I'm tired. My body, mind, and spirit are weary. But even in my exhaustion, thank You for being my strength when I have none left. Help me to rest in Your presence, trusting that I don't have to perform for Your approval. Remind me that true strength isn't just pressing on, but reaching out. I've given all I have, and now I hand the rest to You. Thank You for reminding me that finishing faithful, and helping others finish, is just as beautiful as finishing strong and receiving the victor's trophy. Amen.

———————— † ————————

24. Hope

"We have this hope as an anchor for the soul, firm and secure." - *Hebrews 6:19 (NIV)*
"May the God of hope fill you with all joy and peace as you trust in Him, so that you may overflow with hope by the power of the Holy Spirit." - *Romans 15:13 (NIV)*
"'For I know the plans I have for you,' declares the Lord, 'plans to prosper you and not to harm you, plans to give you hope and a future.'" - *Jeremiah 29:11 (NIV)*

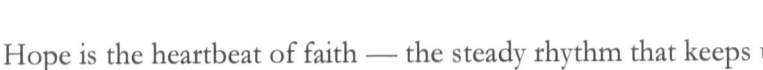

Hope is the heartbeat of faith — the steady rhythm that keeps us moving forward when everything around us feels heavy. It's the whisper that says, *"Don't give up — God's not finished."*

Last night, I hosted a Gratitude Party at Celebrate Recovery — the second year in a row. The Lord laid it on my heart last year because I could see how deeply people wrestle with their hurts, habits, and hang-ups. Week after week, they face their pain and brokenness with courage — but I felt the Lord say, *"They need a night to breathe. A night to praise Me. A night to remember that there is still hope."*

Because sometimes, even in our healing journey, we forget what we're healing toward. Hope reminds us that the pain isn't permanent, the story isn't over, and the same God who brought us through yesterday is already working in our tomorrow.

When I think about hope, I picture a lighthouse on a stormy night. The waves crash, the wind howls, and visibility is almost gone — but that light keeps shining through the darkness. It doesn't make the storm stop; it simply reminds the sailors there's still a way home. That's what God's hope does for us — it anchors us when life tries to toss us around.

Hebrews 6:19 calls hope "an anchor for the soul, firm and secure." Not an anchor that drags us down, but one that holds us steady.

Romans 15:13 says that the God of hope fills us with joy and peace as we trust Him. Hope and trust go hand in hand — the more we trust, the more room He has to fill us.

And Jeremiah 29:11 reminds us that His plans always hold purpose. Even when the path feels uncertain, hope whispers that His promises are still true.

That's what Gratitude night was about: giving thanks not just for what God has done, but for what He's still doing. Because every moment of gratitude grows into hope. Every song of praise plants a seed for tomorrow's miracle.

So when life feels dark — when you're tempted to think you've run out of hope — look back on how far He's already brought you. You're still here. And that means He's not finished yet.

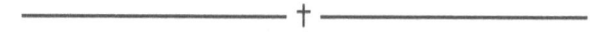

Takeaway:
Hope isn't the denial of pain, it's the declaration that pain doesn't get the final word.

Question for Reflection:
What's one area of your life that needs the reminder that God's not done yet? Carry an "attitude of gratitude" by listing three things you are grateful for today.

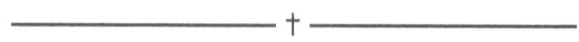

Prayer:

Lord, thank You for being the God of hope. Thank You for meeting me in the dark places and reminding me that Your light never fades even in the most turbulent of storms. Fill me with renewed hope today, hope that anchors my heart, lifts my spirit, and fuels my praise. Help me to remember that no matter what I face, You've already written redemption into my story. Amen.

——————————— † ———————————

25. Waiting on God

"Be still before the Lord and wait patiently for Him; do not fret when people succeed in their ways, when they carry out their wicked schemes." - *Psalm 37:7 (NIV)*

"Wait for the Lord; be strong and take heart and wait for the Lord." - *Psalm 27:14 (NIV)*

"But those who hope in the Lord will renew their strength. They will soar on wings like eagles; they will run and not grow weary, they will walk and not be faint." - *Isaiah 40:31 (NIV)*

"The Lord is good to those whose hope is in Him, to the one who seeks Him." - *Lamentations 3:25 (NIV)*

———————————— † ————————————

Waiting on God can feel like standing in a hallway after every door has closed. You knock, you pray, you listen — and still, silence. You know He's there, but it feels like He's not moving, not answering, not doing anything.

We talk a lot about faith, but not as much about patience, yet patience is faith stretched over time. It's easy to trust when God is working fast and we can see His hand at work in our lives, but the challenge is trusting when we don't see Him moving at all.

Waiting on God is like standing at an intersection, waiting for the WALK sign to turn green. When traffic rushes by, you know it's not safe to move. But when the streets are empty and the light still won't change, that's when it's hardest to wait. Impatience creeps in. Doubt whispers, "Maybe I should just go." Yet that's when trust is proven — when you stay still until God says, "Go."

Waiting requires surrender of control, of timing, and even understanding. We want answers now, healing now, and outcomes now. But God's timing is never random or late. Sometimes His delays are divine protection. Sometimes He's preparing the path ahead of you. And most often, He's preparing *you*.

Waiting often invites you to dig deeper into Him: into His Word, His presence, and His peace. The mountain you face might still loom in front of you because He's strengthening the climber. Waiting shifts your focus from what you want to what He's trying to build within you.

When I think about waiting, I picture a seed buried deep in potting soil. It looks like nothing is happening, but beneath the surface, roots are forming in the dark, invisible to the one waiting for the sprout to break the through the surface of the soil. Without those roots, there won't be the lively growth we've been waiting for. That's what waiting does. It anchors you when you can't see God's plan for your future.

Still, waiting seasons can ache. You may feel overlooked, forgotten, or stuck — watching others move ahead while you stand still. But silence isn't absence. God hasn't forgotten you. He's simply growing something that takes time to burst through the darkness and into the light.

Psalm 27:14 reminds us, "Wait for the Lord; be strong and take heart." Waiting doesn't mean weakness; it means courage. Isaiah 40:31 promises that those who hope in the Lord will renew their strength — not lose it. And Lamentations 3:25 assures us that "the Lord is good to those whose hope is in Him." God isn't ignoring your wait; He's honoring it.

———————— † ————————

Takeaway:
God's delays aren't denials. What feels like stillness is often sacred space — where faith takes root, courage is built, and strength is renewed.

Question for Reflection:
What have you been praying for that hasn't happened yet, and how might God be using this waiting season to strengthen your trust and draw you closer to Him?

————————————— † —————————————

————————————— † —————————————

When You Need Peace And Joy Restored

There are seasons when the storm finally quiets — but peace still feels far away.
You've survived the chaos, but the calm feels strange. You know you should feel grateful,
but instead, you feel hollow.

That's when God whispers, *"Be still — I'm not just calming the storm around you.*
I'm healing the one within you."

This section is for the moments when your soul longs for peace but your mind won't rest,
when joy feels out of reach, and gratitude feels forced.
It's for the days when worship feels heavy instead of holy —
and for the nights when you just need to remember that God hasn't forgotten how to rejoice over you.

Peace and joy aren't feelings you have to chase;
they're promises you can rest in, and gifts that grow in the quiet places where God restores what the world has worn down.

———————————— † ————————————

26. Peace

"Peace I leave with you; My peace I give you. I do not give to you as the world gives. Do not let your hearts be troubled and do not be afraid." - *John 14:27 (NIV)*
"You will keep in perfect peace those whose minds are steadfast, because they trust in You." - *Isaiah 26:3 (NIV)*
"The Lord gives strength to His people; the Lord blesses His people with peace." - *Psalm 29:11 (NIV)*

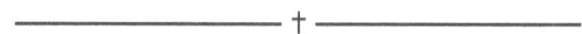

Peace — it's the one thing we all crave but can't seem to hold onto for long. The world teaches us to chase peace through control, completion, or comfort, but the peace God offers doesn't depend on circumstance. God's peace is deeper, steadier, and rooted in His presence, not our perfection.

After a long season of striving and exhaustion, I've realized how often I confuse *quiet* with *peace*. Quiet is the absence of noise; peace is the presence of God. Quiet can be interrupted, but peace remains even when the world gets loud again.

When I think about peace, I picture a calm lake at sunrise. The surface of the water is glassy and still, the light just beginning to touch the water in the cool of the early morning, everything reflecting in harmony. That's what peace in Christ feels like: a settled stillness that doesn't deny life's chaos, but rests in the hands that hold it.

Isaiah 26:3 promises that God keeps in perfect peace those whose minds are steadfast — not those whose lives are flawless, but those who trust Him enough to stop trying to control everything. Sometimes the biggest battle isn't around us, it's the one raging within us.

John 14:27 reminds us that Jesus gives *His* peace — not a substitute or temporary calm, but the same peace that carried Him through storms, betrayal, and even the cross. The peace Christ gives us is unshakable because it isn't based on us — it's based on Him.

And Psalm 29:11 declares that God blesses His people with peace. It's not something we fight for or earn; it's a gift freely given.

So maybe peace isn't about doing more — maybe it's about being still long enough to receive what's already been offered. To pause, breathe, and let God remind you that He's not asking you to calm the storm — He's asking you to trust the One who can.

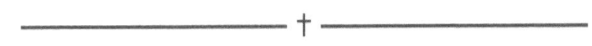

Takeaway:
Peace isn't found in escaping life's noise and turmoil: it's found in inviting God into the middle of it.

Question for Reflection:
What would it look like for you to stop chasing temporary peace and simply rest in the truth that God has already given it to you despite the storm?

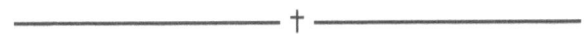

Prayer:
Lord, I'm tired of grasping at peace in places that never satisfy. Help me stop striving and start resting in You. Quiet my mind, calm my heart, and remind me that true peace isn't the absence of chaos — it's the presence of Christ. Thank You for offering a peace the world can't take away. Help me walk in that peace daily and carry it wherever I go. Amen.

27. Joy

"…The joy of the Lord is your strength." - *Nehemiah 8:10 (NIV)*
"Though you have not seen Him, you love Him; and even though you do not see Him now, you believe in Him and are filled with an inexpressible and glorious joy." - *1 Peter 1:8 (NIV)*
"Rejoice in the Lord always. I will say it again: Rejoice!" - *Philippians 4:4 (NIV)*

— † —

Joy isn't always loud. It doesn't always come with laughter, dancing, or easy days. Sometimes joy is quiet, a steady flame that keeps burning, even when the wind howls.

For a long time, I thought joy meant constant smiles and positivity. But I've learned that joy isn't built on circumstances — it's built on confidence in Who holds my circumstances.

Nehemiah 8:10 says, "The joy of the Lord is your strength," not the joy of success, nor the joy of everything going right, but the *joy of the Lord.* That kind of joy doesn't depend on what's happening around you, rather it's born from what's happening within you.

There have been days when life felt heavy, when I was weary, hurting, or unsure what was to come next, yet somewhere deep in my spirit, I still felt peace. I still found reasons to smile. I still heard that gentle whisper saying, "You're going to be okay." That's joy.

When I think about it, joy is like a sunflower. No matter which direction the storm comes from, it keeps turning its face toward the light. A sunflower doesn't deny the rain or the wind — it simply keeps reaching for the sun.

1 Peter 1:8 calls it "inexpressible and glorious joy." That's the kind of joy that doesn't always make sense, but the kind that shines brightest in the darkest valleys.

Paul wrote from prison, "Rejoice in the Lord always. I will say it again: Rejoice!" (Philippians 4:4). His body was chained, but his spirit wasn't. That's the difference between happiness and joy. The feeling of happiness is fleeting, but pure joy is rooted too deep in faith to be stolen by circumstance.

Real joy is knowing that even when life hurts, God is still good. Even when you can't see the end, He's still faithful. Joy is what reminds your soul that you are loved, chosen, and never forgotten — even on those hard days.

———————————— † ————————————

Takeaway:
Joy isn't the absence of trouble — it's the presence of God.

Question for Reflection:
What are the small things that bring you joy? Are there quiet reminders that God is still good in your life even when the rain comes?

———————————— † ————————————

Prayer:
Lord, thank You for joy that runs deeper than happiness; for the kind of joy that anchors my heart even in the storm. Teach me to find joy in Your presence, in Your promises, and in Your unshakable love. Help me to turn my face toward You, like a sunflower toward the sun, and let Your light fill my soul with joy that never fades. Amen.

———————————— † ————————————

28. Gratitude

"Give thanks to the Lord, for He is good; His love endures forever."
- *Psalm 107:1 (NIV)*
"Give thanks to the Lord, for He is good. His love endures forever."
- *Psalm 136:1 (NIV)*
"Therefore, since we are receiving a kingdom that cannot be shaken, let us be thankful, and so worship God acceptably with reverence and awe." - *Hebrews 12:28 (NIV)*

True gratitude isn't about everything being perfect — it's about recognizing that even in the imperfect, God is still good.

It's easy to be thankful when blessings are visible and prayers are being answered. But real gratitude goes deeper. It's what rises up when you can't yet see what God is doing, but you choose to trust that He's doing something.

Gratitude isn't denial — it's declaration. Gratitude is standing in the middle of uncertainty and saying, *"Lord, I thank You anyway."* It's remembering that His goodness isn't proven by what's happening in your life — it's proven by who He's always been.

Psalm 136:1 says, "Give thanks to the Lord, for He is good. His love endures forever." Gratitude begins there — in remembering that God's love doesn't expire when circumstances change. And Hebrews 12:28 reminds us that our thankfulness isn't a fleeting emotion; it's worship. When we thank God even in the struggle, we acknowledge His sovereignty and steady our hearts in His unshakable kingdom.

Gratitude in hardship is faith in motion — a declaration that no matter what comes, God is still worthy of praise.

When I think about gratitude, I think about how often God is working behind the scenes — arranging, protecting, redirecting — in ways we may never know. Sometimes what feels like silence is actually strategy. God is positioning things for your good long before you ever see it. And that alone is reason enough to say, *thank You.*

Gratitude shifts our focus from what we lack to Who we have. It reminds us that God doesn't owe us anything, yet He gives us everything that truly matters — mercy, grace, strength, and unconditional love.

Even when we don't feel Him, He's there. Even when we don't understand His plan, He's working. Gratitude is how we keep our hearts aligned with His — not because life is perfect, but because He is.

———————————— † ————————————

Takeaway:
Gratitude isn't built on what you see — it's rooted in who God is. When you thank Him in the waiting, the worrying, and the wondering, peace begins to fill the space where doubt once lived.

Question for Reflection:
What areas of your life feel uncertain right now — and how can you shift your focus from what you can't see to the faithfulness of God you know is there?

———————————— † ————————————

Prayer:

Lord, thank You — not just for what You've done, but for who You are. Thank You for working in ways I can't always see and for holding things together even when I feel like they're falling apart. Teach me to live with a heart of gratitude that doesn't depend on circumstances, but on Your unchanging goodness. Let my thankfulness be an act of worship, rooted in reverence and awe of who You are. Even in the midst of life's storms, help me to lift my hands and sing with joy to You. Amen.

———————————— † ————————————

29. Love

"A new command I give you: Love one another. As I have loved you, so you must love one another." - *John 13:34 (NIV)*
"Do everything in love." - *1 Corinthians 16:14 (NIV)*
"Above all, love each other deeply, because love covers over a multitude of sins." - *1 Peter 4:8 (NIV)*

———————— † ————————

The word *love* gets used in so many different ways.

We say we love our families and our friends — but we also say we love spaghetti, rainy days, and mountain getaways. (For me, it's my mom's chocolate raisin cake!)

But if we're honest, those don't hit the same. There's a big difference between loving dessert and loving someone deeply. The love we feel for people carries weight — emotion, sacrifice, and connection.

And even that love — as beautiful and meaningful as it is — still doesn't compare to the love God has for us.

God's love is unlike anything we can fully understand. It's wider than the oceans, deeper than our sin, and stronger than our failures. It's the kind of love that doesn't just say, *"I care about you."* It says, *"I'll die for you."*

Jesus said in John 13:34, "As I have loved you, so you must love one another." That kind of love isn't based on convenience or comfort. It's selfless, intentional, and often costly. It's the love that goes first — even when the other person doesn't deserve it.

1 Peter 4:8 reminds us, "Love each other deeply, because love covers over a multitude of sins." That doesn't mean love ignores wrongdoing — it means love chooses grace over judgment. It's a reminder that love heals what hate divides.

When I think about love in action, I picture a candle lighting another candle. The first flame doesn't lose anything by sharing its light — it multiplies the glow. That's what love does. It doesn't run out. It expands, warms, and invites others to shine.

And love isn't just for the easy moments or the lovable people. It's for the coworker who snaps at you when you're being kind. It's for the stranger who cuts you off in traffic.
It's even for the family member who's hurt you more than once.
Because love isn't just a feeling — it's a reflection of God Himself.

Maybe the reason *love* is used in so many different ways is because it's the language of life. Everything meaningful — everything truly good — begins and ends with love.

———————— † ————————

Takeaway:
Love isn't something you fall into — it's something you live out. When you love others the way God loves you, your life becomes a reflection of His heart.

Question for Reflection:
How can you show someone God's love today — not just through words, but through kindness, grace, and genuine care?

———————— † ————————

Prayer:
Lord, thank You for loving me with a love that is deeper, stronger, and greater than anything I can comprehend. Teach me to love others like You love me — with patience, mercy, and sincerity. Help my words and actions reflect Your heart so others can feel Your presence through me today. Amen.

———————— † ————————

30. Worship

"God is spirit, and His worshipers must worship in the Spirit and in truth." - *John 4:24 (NIV)*
"Let everything that has breath praise the Lord." - *Psalm 150:6 (NIV)*
"I will bless the Lord at all times; His praise will always be on my lips." - *Psalm 34:1 (NIV)*

Worship isn't just the songs we sing on Sunday mornings — it's the posture of our hearts every day of the week.

It's easy to think worship only happens when the music swells, the lights dim, and hands are raised high. But worship is so much deeper than that. Worship is how we live, how we speak, how we love, and how we respond when life gets heavy.

I'll be honest — I am not a physical worshiper. What does that mean? Well, if you see me in church on a Sunday morning, I'm the one sitting quietly in my chair during the loudest, most upbeat songs, surrounded by people standing, dancing, swaying, and clapping. That's just not me. And that's OK! For me, Sundays are for serious, reverent prayer and reflection.

And when I first saw people using worship fans? My first thought was, *"What is this ridiculousness?!"*

But today, I get it. And I rejoice in their worship.

There's no one "right" way to worship God. Some people worship through stillness, others through movement. Some pour their hearts out through song, while others express devotion through quiet reverence, service, or gratitude.

Outside of church, especially during our Gratitude Parties at Celebrate Recovery, I can get physical. I can get bouncy. I've even been known to wave a worship flag or two!

And you know what? That's worship, too.

Because true worship isn't about what your body does physically, it's about what your heart is doing.

John 4:24 says we must worship "in Spirit and in truth." That means worship comes from the inside out — from an honest, living connection with God. Whether you're sitting in silence or dancing in joy, if your heart is turned toward Him, it's worship.

When I think of worship, I picture standing in the middle of a storm with my hands raised anyway. Worship doesn't always change the situation, but it always changes me. It reminds me who's in control, who's faithful, and who's worthy — no matter what I'm facing.

Psalm 34:1 says, "I will bless the Lord at all times." Not just in the good times, not just when the music moves us, but *at all times.*

That's the beauty of worship — it's as unique as our relationship with God Himself. Whether your worship is quiet or loud, still or moving, private or public — every act of sincere praise draws us closer to Him.

———————— † ————————

Takeaway:
Worship isn't about how it looks — it's about Who it's for. Whether you're waving a flag or whispering a prayer, if your heart is turned toward God, that's true worship.

Question for Reflection:
What form of worship feels most natural for you — and how might God be inviting you to experience Him in new ways?

———————— † ————————

Prayer:

Lord, thank You for reminding me that worship isn't a performance — it's a connection. Whether I sit in stillness or dance in joy, let my heart stay focused on You. Teach me to worship in Spirit and in truth, and to honor You in every expression — quiet or loud, simple or extravagant. You are always worthy of my praise. Amen.

———————— † ————————

31. Illness / Pain

"He heals the brokenhearted and binds up their wounds." - *Psalm 147:3 (NIV)*
"…My grace is sufficient for you, for My power is made perfect in weakness." - *2 Corinthians 12:9 (NIV)*
"The Lord sustains them on their sickbed and restores them from their bed of illness." - *Psalm 41:3 (NIV)*

———————————— † ————————————

Pain has a way of silencing everything around it. When you're in it — physically, emotionally, or spiritually — it becomes hard to hear anything else, even God's voice.

Whether it's a chronic illness, an unexpected diagnosis, or the weariness of yet another hospital visit, pain tests both our endurance and our faith. It leaves us asking questions that don't always have answers.

And sometimes, the hardest part isn't the pain itself — it's the waiting for relief, the wondering if God still sees you, if He's still listening, if healing will ever come.

This year, I've been fighting a long, exhausting battle with kidney stones.
I've had stents put in, lithotripsies done, and more blockages and complications than I can count. There have been nights when I've curled up in pain so intense it left me breathless, or found myself so sick from pain-induced vomiting that I could barely whisper a prayer.

And yet, through all of it, people around me have continued to pray — and I've continued to believe.

Because I *know* the Lord can heal me. I know He has the power to make this all stop in an instant. But I also know His timing is perfect — and sometimes, there's a purpose in the pain.

Sometimes it's someone I'm meant to meet along the way.
Sometimes it's something I'm meant to learn about endurance, humility, or compassion.
Sometimes it's about deepening my faith in a way I couldn't if everything was easy.

But I'll be honest — in those moments when the pain is blinding and the exhaustion is overwhelming, it's hard to remember that. It's hard to cling to God when every nerve in your body is screaming.

And yet, that's when it matters most.

It's when I lean *into* Him — not away from Him — that true healing begins.

2 Corinthians 12:9 reminds us, *"My grace is sufficient for you, for My power is made perfect in weakness."* The miracle isn't always in the cure — maybe it's in the strength He gives us to keep going. The healing isn't only physical — maybe it's spiritual, emotional, and eternal.

Psalm 41:3 says, *"The Lord sustains them on their sickbed."*
That word — sustains — means He's not just watching from a distance. He's actively holding us together when our bodies and hearts feel like they're falling apart.

When I think about illness and pain now, I picture a storm I can't control but can learn to rest in. The waves may crash, but Jesus is still in the boat — and He hasn't once let me sink.

———————————— † ————————————

Takeaway:
Healing doesn't always come the way we expect — sometimes it comes through patient endurance, a different perspective, and the deep peace of knowing God is in control even when our bodies aren't.

Question for Reflection:
Where in your pain can you see God sustaining you? Even if the healing hasn't come yet, how is God's grace sufficient?

——————————— † ———————————

Prayer:
Lord, You see every ache, every moment of weakness, every tear cried in the middle of the night. You know the pain I've carried and the prayers I've whispered. Thank You for being present in the waiting, for sustaining me when I can't stand on my own. I know You can heal me — but until You do, teach me to find purpose in the pain and to cling to You with all that I am. Let Your grace be enough for today. Amen.

——————————— † ———————————

32. Depression / Sadness

"The Lord is close to the brokenhearted and saves those who are crushed in spirit." - *Psalm 34:18 (NIV)*
"Why, my soul, are you downcast? Why so disturbed within me? Put your hope in God, for I will yet praise Him, my Savior and my God." - *Psalm 42:11 (NIV)*
"The light shines in the darkness, and the darkness has not overcome it." - *John 1:5 (NIV)*

Before I was rescued by Christ, I battled severe bipolar depression. I'd run the full course of antidepressants, therapy, and treatment plans, but nothing seemed to make a lasting difference. My doctor was even at the point of recommending electroshock therapy. While today's process is far gentler than the old horror movie versions, it still carries a risk of memory loss. As a 911 operator and dispatcher, I couldn't afford to lose my memory - the safety of others depends upon it.

So I just kept pushing through.

Even after Jesus saved me, the heaviness didn't completely disappear. It eased, yes, but I still found myself sinking under the weight of sadness at times, wondering why freedom didn't always feel... free.

It wasn't until I went through deliverance that I finally understood the depth of what I'd been fighting all those years.

Depression isn't just a chemical imbalance or a bad day — it is also spiritual warfare. The enemy works overtime to keep you from walking fully in your purpose, to keep you focused on your pain instead of your calling.

Once that veil lifted, I began to see the truth: depression is one of the enemy's favorite weapons because it clouds our vision and silences our prayer life. When you're weighed down by despair, it's hard to even lift your head toward Heaven, let alone call out to God for help.

But the moment you do — the moment you whisper His name — light breaks through the darkness.

Even today, I still face moments when that heaviness tries to creep back in. I still have days when sadness lingers and the old shadows try to whisper lies. But they don't own me anymore.

Because now, I can recognize the tactics of the enemy for what they are, and I can fight back with faith.

I can call out the enemy for his schemes, rebuke the darkness in Jesus' name, and rise faster than before. The difference isn't that I never feel low — it's that I no longer live there.

Psalm 42:11 says, "Put your hope in God, for I will yet praise Him." That word *yet* is powerful. It means there's still a song coming, still hope ahead, still light breaking through.

The enemy tried to bury me in despair, but he didn't realize I was a seed.
And God had every intention of watching me grow.

——————————— † ———————————

Takeaway:
Depression may whisper defeat, but God declares victory. Even in the darkest moments, His light never stops shining — and neither should yours.

Question for Reflection:
When sadness or depression tries to take hold, what truth from God's Word can you hold onto to remind yourself that the darkness will not win?

--------------------- † ---------------------

Prayer:

Father, thank You for meeting me in my lowest places and reminding me that even there, Your light still shines. When depression tries to return, help me to see it for what it is — the enemy's attempt to silence what You've started in me. Strengthen me to fight back with Your Word and to keep walking in freedom. Thank You for deliverance, for healing, and for the peace that can only come from You. Amen.

--------------------- † ---------------------

33. Loss / Grief

"The Lord is close to the brokenhearted and saves those who are crushed in spirit." - *Psalm 34:18 (NIV)*

"Blessed are those who mourn, for they shall be comforted." - *Matthew 5:4 (NIV)*

"He will wipe every tear from their eyes. There will be no more death or mourning or crying or pain, for the old order of things has passed away." - *Revelation 21:4 (NIV)*

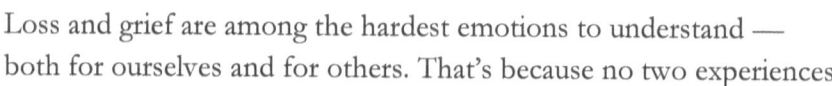

Loss and grief are among the hardest emotions to understand — both for ourselves and for others. That's because no two experiences of grief are ever the same.

For some, it comes in waves of tears and heartbreak. For others, it shows up as numbness, anger, or even relief.

When my father passed away in 1994, I didn't cry. There was no breakdown, no dramatic moment of mourning. Instead, I felt relief — a heavy burden I didn't even realize I was still carrying had lifted. I even wanted to watch the funeral home attendants take his body from the house, not out of cruelty, but for closure. A part of me needed to see with my own eyes that he was truly gone — that the pain, the fear, and the hurt tied to him were finally over.

But when my mother passed in 2015, grief hit differently. Harder. Deeper. I spiraled so intensely that I admitted myself to the hospital because I simply didn't know how to keep breathing through the pain.

Two parents. Two losses. Two completely different responses.

That's the thing about grief: it doesn't follow rules, norms, or timelines. It's not something you "get over." It's something you *walk through,* moment by moment, learning how to carry both love and loss at the same time.

Even now, as a parent, I sometimes find myself worrying about how I would react if I ever had to face that kind of loss again — especially if it involved one of my children. It's a thought that steals your breath, one you instantly hand to God because it's too heavy to hold alone.

And that's what we're meant to do in our grief — lean into God.

He's not afraid of our tears. He's not offended by our anger. He's not disappointed in our confusion. He simply holds us — close enough to feel His heartbeat when ours feels broken.

Psalm 34:18 reminds us, "The Lord is close to the brokenhearted and saves those who are crushed in spirit." Grief doesn't scare God away — it draws Him closer.

And Matthew 5:4 promises comfort to those who mourn — not instant healing, not immediate peace, but the kind of comfort that slowly wraps around your soul and whispers, *"You're not alone."*

It's easier said than done, of course. When the ache feels unbearable, faith feels fragile. But even in the depths of sorrow, God's presence never wavers.

God is there — in the silence, in the sobs, in the moments when you can't pray.
He's there when your grief looks nothing like anyone else's.
And one day, He'll fulfill the promise of Revelation 21:4 — to wipe away every tear and end the pain once and for all.

Until then, keep leaning in. Keep breathing. Keep holding His hand. Because even when it feels like everything's gone, you're not.

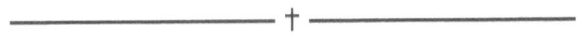

Takeaway:
Grief doesn't look the same for everyone, but God meets each of us right where we are — in the tears, in the relief, in the silence — and walks us toward healing, one breath at a time.

Question for Reflection:
What kind of grief have you carried — and how has God met you in it, even if only in small, quiet ways?

———————————— † ————————————

Prayer:
Father, thank You for being close to the brokenhearted. For understanding the pain of loss in all its forms — the weeping, the numbness, the relief, and the longing. Help me to remember that grief doesn't mean You've left me, but that You're walking with me through it. Wrap Your peace around every heart that's hurting and remind us that Your comfort is constant, even in the chaos of loss.
Amen.

———————————— † ————————————

34. Financial Struggles

"And my God will meet all your needs according to the riches of His glory in Christ Jesus." - *Philippians 4:19 (NIV)*
"Therefore do not worry, saying, 'What shall we eat?' or 'What shall we drink?' or 'What shall we wear?'... For your heavenly Father knows that you need all these things." - *Matthew 6:31–32 (NKJV)*
"...The Lord will provide." - *Genesis 22:14 (NIV)*

———————————— † ————————————

One of the most common phrases we hear as followers of Christ is, *"The Lord will provide."*
But when money is tight and every penny squeaks from being pinched so hard, that promise can be difficult to cling to.

When rent is due, when the fridge is nearly empty, when the car payment looms larger than the balance in your bank account — the idea of "just trusting God" can feel more like pressure than peace.

You want to believe. You *do* believe.
But you also can't ignore the very real anxiety of not knowing how you'll make it through the week.

I've been there more times than I can count — staring at bills, trying to stretch a dollar into three, and wondering if maybe I'd somehow fallen out of God's favor because things were so hard.

And then, just when I'd reached my breaking point, something would happen.
A surprise bonus.
A random refund.
Someone handing me a little extra, saying, "God put this on my heart to give you."

That wasn't coincidence — it was *provision*.

Not because I'm special or because I have it all together.
But because I'm a soldier in His army, taking on battles in His name
— fighting spiritual wars that most people never see.

And God takes care of His soldiers.

The enemy loves to attack us through our finances because he knows
the stress of lack can shake even the strongest faith. But when we
choose to keep trusting God anyway — to stay faithful in the famine
— we become living testimonies of God's goodness.

Matthew 6 reminds us not to worry about what we'll eat, drink, or
wear because our Father already knows what we need. That doesn't
mean He always delivers on *our* timeline, but it does mean His
provision never fails.

Philippians 4:19 promises, "My God will meet all your needs
according to the riches of His glory."
Notice it says *needs,* not *wants.*

Sometimes His provision looks like a promotion, but other times it
looks like the gas tank that somehow lasts longer than it should, or
the neighbor who shows up with groceries right when the pantry
shelves are empty.

Provision doesn't always show up how we expect — but it *always*
shows up.

And when it does, it reminds us that God is still in control, still
faithful, and still providing — even when the numbers don't add up.

———————————— † ————————————

Takeaway:
God's math doesn't have to make sense for His provision to be real.
When you trust Him with your finances, He supplies more than
enough — often in ways you could never predict.

Question for Reflection:

When has God surprised you with provision right when you needed it most? How did that strengthen your trust in Him for the next storm?

———————————— † ————————————

Prayer:

Jehovah Jireh — my Provider — thank You for always coming through, even when I can't see how. Help me to remember that my security doesn't come from my paycheck but from Your promises. When the stress of bills or lack weighs heavy on my heart, help me remember every time You've provided before. Strengthen my faith to keep giving, keep trusting, and keep believing that You are more than enough. Amen.

———————————— † ————————————

35. Purpose in Suffering

"And we know that in all things God works for the good of those who love Him, who have been called according to His purpose." - *Romans 8:28 (NIV)*
"For our light and momentary troubles are achieving for us an eternal glory that far outweighs them all." - *2 Corinthians 4:17 (NIV)*
"The Lord is close to the brokenhearted and saves those who are crushed in spirit." - *Psalm 34:18 (NIV)*

They say, *"There's a method to the madness."*
But when you're in the middle of suffering, seeing that method — that purpose — in the madness feels nearly impossible.

How can a child being abused have a purpose?
How can someone dying young fulfill one?
How can a loving God allow bad things to happen to His people in the name of "purpose"?

These are questions that ache deep in the soul — questions no easy answer can soothe. But over time, through both my pain and my healing, I've come to see that there *is* purpose in suffering.

Picture a lonely lit candle in a room. Left unattended, the candle will eventually sputter out. God's light, shining within His people, needs fuel to keep burning, just like that unattended candle.

That fuel isn't always joy or comfort or success. Sometimes it's pain. Sometimes it's tears. Sometimes it's those long, silent seasons when all you can do is cling to hope.

There's no better fuel for keeping God's light burning than the experiences that nearly extinguished it.

Suffering refines us. It softens our hardened hearts. It helps us see others through God's eyes of empathy and hearts of compassion.

As a pastoral counselor, I sometimes struggle when working with individuals battling substance abuse — not because I don't want to help, but because that's not a pain I've lived. I can't speak that language from experience.

But when it comes to those who have suffered childhood maltreatment or adverse childhood experiences? That I understand. Because I've been there. I've lived that pain. And because I survived, I can meet someone in their darkest moment and say, *"I know this place. You're not alone here."*

That's purpose.

God doesn't cause our suffering — but He does redeem it. He turns pain into purpose and wounds into witness.

Romans 8:28 reminds us that "in all things, God works for the good."
Notice it doesn't say all things *are* good — just that God works them *for* good.

Pain, loss, trauma — they're not good things. But they can become the soil where good things grow.

If your suffering has ever made you feel forgotten or punished, take heart. God isn't wasting a single tear. He's using every ounce of pain to prepare you — to equip you for the purpose only you can fulfill.

Because the light that burns through pain shines the brightest in the darkness.

———————————— † ————————————

Takeaway:
God doesn't cause all things, but He uses all things — even suffering — to shape our purpose and reveal His glory through us.

Question for Reflection:
What pain or hardship in your life might God be transforming into fuel for your light? In what ways can you help someone else find theirs?

———————— † ————————

———————— † ————————

36. Spiritual Dryness

"As the deer pants for streams of water, so my soul pants for You, my God." - *Psalm 42:1 (NIV)*
"For I will pour water on the thirsty land, and streams on the dry ground." - *Isaiah 44:3 (NIV)*
"Blessed are those who hunger and thirst for righteousness, for they shall be filled." - *Matthew 5:6 (NKJV)*

Sometimes, even for strong believers, there are moments when God goes silent.
You're left standing at heaven's doorway asking, *"Lord, did You just ghost me?"*

It reminds me of the books I loved to read as a kid — *"Are You There, God? It's Me, Margaret."*
Only now, it's me calling out, *"Are You there, God? It's me again!"*

When those quiet moments stretch into days or weeks, they can shake your confidence — especially if you operate in spiritual gifts. You start wondering if you've done something wrong, if you've somehow upset God, or if He's pulled His presence away to teach you a lesson.

But that's not what these moments are.

They're what I call *Wilderness Moments* — those dry, desert seasons where everything feels empty and directionless. They aren't meant to punish you. You've most likely done nothing wrong — certainly not enough to make God mad.

They're meant to test and train you.

Just as Jesus was tested in the wilderness, these moments are opportunities to draw closer to God — to trust Him faster, turn to Him first, and learn to walk by faith, not by feelings or circumstances.

In these seasons, God is refining your spirit, strengthening your resolve, and deepening your dependence on Him.
He's teaching you that your faith doesn't fade just because your feelings do.

Isaiah 44:3 says, "I will pour water on the thirsty land, and streams on the dry ground."
The dryness is temporary — the draught is making space for something new.
And when that spiritual rain comes, you'll appreciate its refreshment all the more.

So if you're in a wilderness moment right now, keep seeking. Keep knocking. Keep calling out — even if all you can manage is, *"Lord, I miss You."*

Because God is still there.
He hasn't left you — He's just teaching you to find Him in the silence.

———————— † ————————

Takeaway:
Spiritual dryness isn't God's rejection — it's His refinement. The silence isn't punishment; it's preparation for the next outpouring.

Question for Reflection:
How do you respond when God feels silent — and what might He be teaching you in that stillness?

———————— † ————————

Prayer:

Lord, when You seem far away, remind me that You're still right here. Help me to see the silence not as abandonment, but as an invitation to seek You more deeply. In my wilderness moments, teach me to rely on Your Word, to keep knocking on Heaven's door, and to trust that the rain is coming. Amen.

———————————— † ————————————

37. Anxiety

"Do not be anxious about anything, but in every situation, by prayer and petition, with thanksgiving, present your requests to God." - *Philippians 4:6 (NIV)*

"Cast all your anxiety on Him because He cares for you." - *1 Peter 5:7 (NIV)*

"Peace I leave with you; My peace I give you. I do not give to you as the world gives. Do not let your hearts be troubled and do not be afraid." - *John 14:27 (NIV)*

Anxiety is such a sneaky thing. It doesn't always shout — sometimes it whispers.
It can start with a racing thought, a sleepless night, or a feeling of tension you can't quite shake.

It creeps in when life feels uncertain — when bills are stacked too high, when health feels fragile, when relationships feel distant, or when the world feels heavier than your shoulders can bear.

I've learned that anxiety thrives on control. It convinces us that if we just plan harder, think faster, or do more, we can fix what's wrong. But all that does is exhaust us further — and leave us even more anxious when things still don't work out the way we hoped.

Philippians 4:6 tells us not to be anxious, but to bring *everything* — every fear, every burden — to God in prayer. That's not a demand to "just get over it" but an invitation to trade panic for peace.

And one of the most beautiful ways I've seen that truth in action I learned from a Sister in Christ who shared an exercise that changed how I view anxiety.

She told me to picture an empty box sitting at the feet of Jesus. Then, one by one, start placing everything inside that's weighing me down — the kids, the bills, the job, the relationships, the health concerns — every single burden that's been sitting heavy on my chest.

And once it's all in the box? You let go.
You walk away and let Jesus take care of it.
You don't dig through the box again. You don't snatch anything back. You leave it right there — because that's what surrender looks like.

It's such a freeing experience. It helps you breathe again — not because the problems instantly disappear, but because you're no longer carrying them alone.

1 Peter 5:7 reminds us, "Cast all your anxiety on Him because He cares for you." That word *cast* isn't delicate — it means to throw, to release, to hurl your burdens into His hands.

When you truly do that — when you give Him the whole box — peace rushes in to fill the space anxiety once occupied.

And I can tell you firsthand — that kind of peace is real.

Before I was rescued and delivered, I lived in a constant state of anxiety. I relied heavily on medication just to function day to day. The thought of standing in front of a crowd would leave me physically ill — shaking, sweating, unable to speak.

But when I surrendered that anxiety to God and began truly walking with Him, everything changed. I no longer depend on anti-anxiety medication. I can stand confidently in front of large groups and teach His Word without the panic that once consumed me.

That's not because I'm stronger or better than others — it's because God *is*.
Where fear once ruled, faith now reigns.
Where anxiety once crippled me, God's peace now carries me.

--------------------------------- † ---------------------------------

Takeaway:

Anxiety loses its grip when you give your burdens to God instead of trying to balance them yourself. The peace He gives isn't the absence of problems — it's the assurance that He's handling what you can't.

Question for Reflection:

What burdens are you still trying to carry that belong in the box at Jesus' feet?

--------------------------------- † ---------------------------------

Prayer:

Lord, You know the worries that keep me awake and the burdens that weigh on my heart. Today, I'm bringing them to You — every one. Teach me to release them, to trust that You care for me more than I can imagine. Fill me with Your peace where anxiety once lived, and remind me that I was never meant to carry the weight alone. Thank You for the freedom that only comes from You. Amen.

--------------------------------- † ---------------------------------

38. Weariness / Burnout

"Come to me, all you who are weary and burdened, and I will give you rest." - *Matthew 11:28 (NIV)*

———————————— † ————————————

There's a kind of tired that sleep can't fix.
It's the weariness that runs deeper than your bones — the heaviness that settles in your spirit after too many days of holding it all together.

You keep showing up, giving, helping, pushing — but the truth is, you're running on fumes.

When I think of weariness, I imagine being a boxer — stuck in the ring, taking hit after hit, round after round. You're exhausted, beaten down, and ready for the match to end. But sometimes it feels like you don't have anyone in your corner to throw in the towel for you. You just keep swinging, hoping you'll find the strength for one more round.

Burnout doesn't happen overnight: it builds up over time. It creeps in quietly — one *"I'll just handle it"* at a time, one *"they need me"* after another — until suddenly you're running on empty and can't remember the last time you refueled through rest.

Physical exhaustion turns into mental fog. Emotional fatigue seeps into your spiritual life. Even prayer starts to feel heavy.

But Jesus never asked you to keep fighting alone.
He said, *"Come to Me."*

That's not an invitation to perform — it's a call to rest. To breathe. To step out of the ring and let Him tend to your wounds.

Sometimes rest isn't about sleeping more — it's about trusting more. True rest is realizing you don't have to prove your strength to God. You just have to surrender to His.

Because the truth is, your worth isn't measured by your productivity — it's found in His presence.

And when you finally let Him hold you, you'll find that rest was never a reward for finishing the fight. It was a gift waiting for you the whole time.

———————— † ————————

Takeaway:
Rest isn't weakness — it's worship. True rest happens when you stop striving and start surrendering.

Question for Reflection:
Where in your life have you been in the fight, taking hit after hit without stepping out of the ring? What would it look like to let Jesus be the one in your corner today?

———————— † ————————

Prayer:
Lord, I'm weary — in my mind, my body, my emotions, and my spirit. I've been trying to carry too much and keep fighting battles I was never meant to fight alone. Help me to lay down my gloves, step out of the ring, and find my rest in You. Restore my strength, refresh my soul, and renew my joy in serving You. Teach me to breathe again in Your presence. Amen.

———————— † ————————

39. Feeling Overlooked (By People)

"Let us not become weary in doing good, for at the proper time we will reap a harvest if we do not give up." - *Galatians 6:9 (NIV)*

"...Your Father, who sees what is done in secret, will reward you." - *Matthew 6:4 (NIV)*

"...The Lord does not look at the things people look at. People look at the outward appearance, but the Lord looks at the heart." - *1 Samuel 16:7 (NIV)*

Sometimes the hardest part about showing up faithfully is realizing no one seems to notice.

You work hard, love deeply, serve quietly — but the recognition never comes.

Your effort gets overshadowed, your voice goes unheard, your name unmentioned.

It's a lonely kind of ache — to feel invisible in a world that celebrates the loudest, the biggest, the most visible and successful.

When I think about feeling overlooked, I picture a flower blooming in the middle of a forest.

No one walks by to admire its beauty, no camera captures its color — yet it blooms anyway.

It doesn't need an audience; it grows because that's what it was created to do.

But if I'm honest, my biggest struggle in those moments has always been pride.

Pride rears its head when I feel unseen. I can't tell you how many times I've been hurt because a Sister in Christ chose someone else for something I knew I could do. I'd find myself wondering, *"Why not me? Why wasn't I even on her radar?"*

Pride whispers that being unseen means being unworthy — but God gently reminds you that being unseen doesn't mean being unused.

Galatians 6:9 encourages us not to grow weary in doing good, "for at the proper time we will reap a harvest if we do not give up."
Sometimes the recognition we crave isn't meant to come from people — it's meant to come from God.

Matthew 6:4 promises that "Your Father, who sees what is done in secret, will reward you."
He sees every act of obedience, every quiet moment of service, every tear shed in surrender. His validation will always outweigh human applause.

And 1 Samuel 16:7 reminds us that "People look at the outward appearance, but the Lord looks at the heart." God sees motives that others overlook, and sometimes He intentionally hides us for a season — not to punish us, but to purify us.
God teaches us that true service flows from love, not from being seen.

You weren't overlooked — maybe you were *set apart*.
Hidden on purpose.
Because God often grows the strongest roots in unseen soil.

———————————— † ————————————

Takeaway:
Being overlooked doesn't diminish your calling — it refines it. Let God turn the sting of being unseen into the strength of serving from a pure heart.

Question for Reflection:
When pride rises up after being overlooked, how can you redirect that moment toward humility and trust in God's timing?

———————————— † ————————————

Prayer:

Lord, You know how it hurts when I feel invisible — when others are chosen and I'm not. Help me to quiet my pride and remember that You see what no one else does. Remind me that hidden seasons are holy seasons, and that Your timing is perfect. Teach me to serve from a place of humility and love, not for recognition but for You. Amen.

———————————— † ————————————

40. Feeling Unworthy

"See, I have engraved you on the palms of my hands; your walls are ever before me." - *Isaiah 49:16 (NIV)*
"The Lord is close to the brokenhearted and saves those who are crushed in spirit." - *Psalm 34:18 (NIV)*
"She is more precious than rubies; nothing you desire can compare with her." - *Proverbs 3:15 (NIV)*
"But God demonstrates His own love for us in this: While we were still sinners, Christ died for us." - *Romans 5:8 (NIV)*

———————————— † ————————————

When I think about feeling unworthy, I picture Cinderella from *Ever After.*

Born of noble station, she was reduced to servitude by cruelty. She knew she was meant for more — she felt it deep within her bones — yet every voice around her told her otherwise. Day after day, she lived beneath her identity until she started to believe it.

That's what unworthiness feels like. You know you were made for more, but the world — and sometimes even your own thoughts — keep trying to convince you otherwise.

There have been seasons in my life when I felt exactly like that. Like no matter how much I did or how hard I tried, people only saw the servant, not the soul. They saw my flaws, not my faith. They brought up my past, not my potential. And slowly, I started to forget who I was, too.

But here's the truth: God never forgot.

Isaiah 49:16 says, "See, I have engraved you on the palms of my hands."
God doesn't just know you — He carries your name, your story, and

your scars right there with Him. You're not overlooked. You're etched into eternity.

Psalm 34:18 reminds us that "The Lord is close to the brokenhearted."
When you feel unseen, unheard, or unloved, He draws nearer — not farther away. He doesn't wait for you to feel worthy; He meets you right where you are.

And Romans 5:8 declares that "while we were still sinners, Christ died for us."
Before you ever did a thing to earn it. Before you ever "got it together," Jesus decided He would die for you. That's how much He values you.

When I think about Jesus' sacrifice for me, I realize something profound: worthiness isn't about how the world sees me — it's about who God sees me. The same Jesus also sacrificed Himself for you too, because you are worthy.

You are royal blood living in a fallen world. You may feel like the servant in rags, but your Father still sees His child in royal robes.

And when I need that reminder, I have a small tradition I've grown fond of over the years: I've collected a few tiaras in my travels. It might sound silly to some, but when I'm feeling unworthy or forgotten, I put one on and remind myself:
I am a royal, blood-bought daughter of the King of Kings.

There is no title on earth higher than that. And though it's a title I share with millions, His Kingdom is vast and full of glory — there's room enough for us all.

I am a Princess of Heaven, and no one has the power or authority to strip that from me. Proverbs 3:15 says I am "more precious than rubies," and that truth will always outshine any lie the world throws my way.

---
†

Takeaway:

You are not who others say you are. You are who God created you to be — loved, chosen, seen, and crowned with worth that cannot be taken away.

Question for Reflection:

What small, tangible reminder could you use — like a tiara, ring, or note — to help you remember who you are in Christ when the world tries to make you forget?

---
†

Prayer:

Lord, there are days I feel like Cinderella — unseen, unworthy, and overlooked. But You see me. You remind me that I am Your daughter — royal, redeemed, and more precious than rubies. Help me to walk with the quiet confidence of a Princess of Heaven, not because of what I've done, but because of who You are. Thank You for calling me worthy when I felt worthless. Amen.

---
†
---

41. Loneliness

"Be strong and courageous. Do not be afraid or terrified because of them, for the Lord your God goes with you; He will never leave you nor forsake you." - *Deuteronomy 31:6 (NIV)*

"The Lord is close to the brokenhearted and saves those who are crushed in spirit." - *Psalm 34:18 (NIV)*

"Never will I leave you; never will I forsake you." - *Hebrews 13:5 (NIV)*

"Turn to me and be gracious to me, for I am lonely and afflicted." - *Psalm 25:16 (NIV)*

--------------------- † ---------------------

Loneliness isn't just about being alone — it's about *feeling* alone. You can be surrounded by people and still feel invisible, unheard, or disconnected. It's that quiet ache in your chest when you realize no one truly sees what you're carrying.

Sometimes loneliness follows loss — a friendship fades, a relationship ends, or life simply shifts. Other times, it creeps in slowly, even when everything looks fine on the outside. You smile, show up, and keep doing the things — but inside, you feel alone.

When I think of loneliness, I picture standing in the middle of a crowded room, but everyone's facing the other direction. You're close enough to hear the noise of conversation, but not close enough to be part of any of them. That's the kind of loneliness that hurts the most — not physical isolation, but emotional separation.

Even David, the "man after God's own heart," cried out in Psalm 25:16, "Turn to me and be gracious to me, for I am lonely and afflicted." Loneliness isn't a sign of weak faith — it's a sign of being human and our desire for community. It reminds us that we were created for connection — both with God and with others.

But here's the truth: you are never truly alone.

Psalm 34:18 promises that "The Lord is close to the brokenhearted." Hebrews 13:5 declares, "Never will I leave you; never will I forsake you."
And Deuteronomy 31:6 repeats that same promise with strength and tenderness — "Be strong and courageous... for the Lord your God goes with you."

God's presence isn't dependent on your feelings — it's anchored in His character.

When you feel unseen, God sees you.
When you feel unheard, God listens.
When you feel forgotten, God remembers.
He's not distant in your loneliness — He's dwelling right there with you, even in the silence.

Sometimes, loneliness is also a sacred invitation — a quiet space where God draws you closer to Himself. He allows the noise to fade so you can finally hear His voice again. It's in the stillness that intimacy with Him deepens, and the emptiness begins to fill with His peace.

You may feel alone right now, but you are never abandoned. You are deeply loved, constantly seen, and wholly held by the One who will never leave your side.

Takeaway:
Loneliness may visit, but it doesn't have to stay. Even when people turn away, God turns toward you — faithfully, gently, and always on time.

Question for Reflection:
What does your loneliness look like right now? How might God be using it to draw you closer to Him instead of leaving you in the dark?

———————— † ————————

Prayer:

Lord, You know the ache of loneliness — You felt it in Gethsemane when even Your friends fell asleep instead of standing by Your side. Thank You for reminding me that You understand what it feels like to be alone. Be near me in my quiet moments. Fill the empty spaces with Your presence and peace. Help me to see that even in my solitude, I'm never abandoned — I'm held by You. Use this season to draw me closer, and help me notice others who might feel alone, too. Amen.

———————— † ————————

42. Conflict (Interpersonal)

"If it is possible, as far as it depends on you, live at peace with everyone." - *Romans 12:18 (NIV)*

"A gentle answer turns away wrath, but a harsh word stirs up anger." - *Proverbs 15:1 (NIV)*

"Blessed are the peacemakers, for they will be called children of God." - *Matthew 5:9 (NIV)*

————————————— † —————————————

Conflict is part of life. Even among believers, personalities clash, misunderstandings arise, and emotions flare. But conflict itself isn't the enemy — how we handle it determines whether it becomes a weapon to inflict hurt or a doorway to healing and reconciliation.

In the heat of disagreement, our natural instinct is to defend, argue, or prove our point. But Proverbs 15:1 reminds us that "A gentle answer turns away wrath." Gentleness doesn't mean weakness; it means strength under control. It's the discipline of choosing peace when pride wants to win.

Romans 12:18 gives both wisdom and freedom: "If it is possible, as far as it depends on you, live at peace with everyone." That means peace doesn't always require agreement — it requires humility. It's not about being right; it's about being righteous. Sometimes living at peace means setting a boundary instead of building a wall.

When I think about interpersonal conflict, I picture a game of tug-of-war — but the other end of the rope is tied to a wall. No matter how hard you pull, you're never going to win. All that energy, all that strain, all that emotional effort — and the rope doesn't move an inch. That's what happens when we try to resolve conflict through control instead of surrender. The harder we pull, the more exhausted we become. The only way to end the struggle is to let go.

Resolution doesn't always look like reconciliation, but it always begins with release — releasing the need to be understood, the need to be right, and the desire to retaliate. God doesn't ask us to control others' actions; He asks us to honor Him through ours.

Conflict handled God's way can become an opportunity for spiritual maturity. It teaches us patience, compassion, and the art of listening more than we speak. True peace doesn't mean avoiding conflict; it means inviting Christ into the middle of it.

Takeaway:
Peace doesn't come from winning the argument — it comes from surrendering the outcome to God.

Question for Reflection:
Is there someone you've been in conflict with who weighs heavy on your heart? What would it look like to lay down your "rope" and let God bring peace, whether through resolution or release?

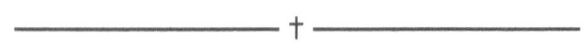

Prayer:
Lord, conflict is hard. It stirs my emotions and tempts me to react instead of respond. Teach me to pause and let Your Spirit guide my words and actions. Help me to pursue peace, not pride — understanding, not victory. Where reconciliation is possible, soften hearts on both sides. And where it's not, help me to release the situation into Your hands and walk away in peace. Make me a peacemaker who reflects Your grace, even in disagreement. Amen.

43. Conflict (With God's Will / Calling)

"Many are the plans in a person's heart, but it is the Lord's purpose that prevails." - *Proverbs 19:21 (NIV)*

"Trust in the Lord with all your heart and lean not on your own understanding; in all your ways submit to Him, and He will make your paths straight." - *Proverbs 3:5–6 (NIV)*

"I desire to do Your will, my God; Your law is within my heart." - *Psalm 40:8 (NIV)*

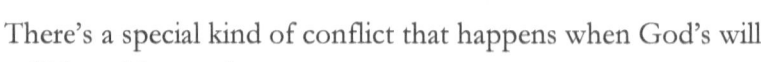

There's a special kind of conflict that happens when God's will collides with our plans.

It's not rebellion — it's wrestling.

We love God, we trust Him, and yet when His direction doesn't match our desire, a quiet battle begins inside: *"Lord, I want Your will… but why does it have to look like this?"*

Conflict with God's will often shows up when the path He's leading us down doesn't make sense — when obedience requires sacrifice, when waiting replaces progress, or when His *"not yet"* feels like *"not ever."* Our hearts want to follow, but our flesh wants to understand.

Proverbs 19:21 reminds us, "Many are the plans in a person's heart, but it is the Lord's purpose that prevails." And that's where the tension lives — between what we plan and what He purposes.

When I think about this kind of conflict, I picture a vending machine. Regrettably, we often treat God like one — we put in our "prayer coin," enter our "blessing request button," and expect our answer to drop instantly for us to enjoy. But waiting on God's timing is like that one stubborn vending machine that takes forever to release your bag of chips. You're standing there, watching, thinking, *"Come on, any second now...*" and just when you think it's about to fall — it gets stuck somewhere in the mechanics of the machine.

You can see the blessing. You know it's right there. But it's just out of reach.

And that's when the urge hits — to shake the machine, knocking it a couple of times for good measure. To take matters into your own hands. To make it happen because we expect immediate results. But imagine how it must look when we do that to God — when we try to force His hand, rush His timing, or demand answers before their season. We're *"shaking the vending machine"* of Heaven.

Thankfully, God's grace is steady even when our patience isn't. But the truth is, our blessings come loose not through force, but through faith.

I've learned that conflict with God's will isn't a sign of weak faith — it's proof that your faith is alive. It's your heart trying to reconcile surrender with self. But the beauty of surrender is that it doesn't require full understanding — just trust.

Sometimes God's will feels like loss before it looks like purpose. Sometimes His calling stretches you in ways that feel uncomfortable or even unfair. But every time you choose obedience over understanding, your spirit grows stronger and your heart grows softer.

Proverbs 3:5–6 teaches us to "trust in the Lord with all your heart and lean not on your own understanding." That's not an easy verse to live — but it's a freeing one. Because when we release our grip on control, we make room for His perfect direction.

God's will doesn't always align with comfort, but it always aligns with goodness. And His calling isn't about perfection — it's about participation. He doesn't need you to understand every step - all He asks you to do is take the next one in faith.

--- † ---

Takeaway:

Conflict with God's will isn't disobedience — it's an invitation to deeper trust. When your plans fall apart, remember: God's purpose never does.

Question for Reflection:

Where are you resisting God's direction or doubting His timing right now? What might change if you trusted that His "no" or "wait" is still leading you somewhere good?

--- † ---

Prayer:

Lord, I don't always understand what You're doing, but I know You're good. Help me trust You when Your will interrupts my plans. When my heart wrestles with obedience, remind me that Your purpose is greater than my comfort. Teach me to let go of the anchors of fear, pride, and control — and to stop trying to "shake" You for answers You're not ready to release. Align my desires with Yours, and give me peace in the process. Amen.

--- † ---

When You're Learning to Walk Free

Freedom in Christ isn't a destination — it's a daily decision.
It's the gentle, courageous act of letting go of what once defined you
and then stepping into who you were always meant to be.

This section isn't about perfection — it's about progression. It's
about learning to recognize sin without shame, to repent without
fear, and to walk forward without the chains that used to hold you
back.

Here, we trade condemnation for conviction, guilt for grace, and
striving for surrender.
Because walking free doesn't mean you'll never stumble again — it
means that when you do, you know whose hand is holding yours as
you rise.

———————— † ————————

44. Recognizing Sin

"If we claim to be without sin, we deceive ourselves and the truth is not in us." - *1 John 1:8 (NIV)*
"For all have sinned and fall short of the glory of God." - *Romans 3:23 (NIV)*
"Surely I was sinful at birth, sinful from the time my mother conceived me." - *Psalm 51:5 (NIV)*

———————————— † ————————————

One of the hardest things for me to hear from fellow Christians used to be, "We're all born in sin."

I couldn't wrap my head around that. How could anyone look at a newborn baby — so small, innocent, and perfect — and declare that child sinful? Psalm 51:5 says, "I was brought forth in iniquity, and in sin did my mother conceive me." But for years, I thought that was just David's personal story — not humanity's.

It took time and a little Holy Spirit clarity before I began to understand what that verse really means. It's not that we're *born in sin* as if God created us broken — it's that we're *born into sin* in a fallen world. Sin isn't something we catch; it's something our human nature drifts toward.

Even children, as innocent as they are, reveal that sinful tendency early on. From the small acts of selfishness, anger, or jealousy that appear almost instinctively. It's not because they're evil; it's because we all have a nature that needs redemption.

Recognizing sin isn't about condemnation or accusation — it's about awareness. It's not meant to shame us but to show us our need for grace. Because until we recognize our sin, we can't fully recognize our Savior who takes it away.

Romans 3:23 reminds us that *"all have sinned and fall short of the glory of God."* That verse isn't meant to punish; it levels the field. It tells us that no one is beyond the reach of mercy.

And 1 John 1:8 says, *"If we claim to be without sin, we deceive ourselves."* Pretending to be perfect doesn't make us holy — it only keeps us from healing and experiencing the forgiveness found only in Christ.

Recognizing sin is less about guilt and more about growth. It's God's way of holding up a mirror — not to embarrass us, but to show us where His grace is still at work. Because once we see sin clearly, we begin to see our need for grace even more clearly too.

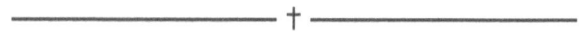

Takeaway:
Recognizing sin isn't about judgment — it's about honesty. God can't heal what we refuse to admit is broken.

Question for Reflection:
Is there an area of your life where you've justified a behavior or mindset that God might be gently calling you to surrender?

Prayer:

Lord, thank You for loving me enough to reveal the places in my heart that still need Your touch. Help me see sin not as a label, but as a reminder of my need for You. Open my eyes to pride, jealousy, anger, or fear — anything that keeps me from reflecting Your love. And when You show me those places, give me the courage to bring them into the light. Thank You that recognition is always met with redemption, and that Your mercy never runs dry. Amen.

45. Repenting from Sin

"If we confess our sins, He is faithful and just and will forgive us our sins and purify us from all unrighteousness." - *1 John 1:9 (NIV)*
"Repent, then, and turn to God, so that your sins may be wiped out, that times of refreshing may come from the Lord." - *Acts 3:19 (NIV)*
"Come to me, all you who are weary and burdened, and I will give you rest." - *Matthew 11:28 (NIV)*

———————————— † ————————————

Like unforgiveness, unrepented sin keeps us from walking in true freedom.

We can feel guilt, remorse, and even sorrow for what we've done — but until we take it to God and repent, we're still carrying the burden. Repentance isn't about groveling before God or trying to earn His forgiveness; it's about releasing what we were never meant to hold in the first place.

When I think about repentance, I picture a hiker carrying a backpack full of rocks he has collected during his journey. Each rock represents a mistake, a wrong choice, a moment of weakness. The hiker adjusts the straps, shift the weight, or tries to distribute the heaviness so he can keep going, but the burden doesn't lessen until he finally set it down. That's what repentance does. It lets us drop the weight of our mistakes at the feet of Jesus.

1 John 1:9 reminds us that when we confess our sins, God is *faithful and just* to forgive us. He's not waiting with judgment — He's waiting with open arms.

Acts 3:19 promises, "Repent... so that times of refreshing may come." Repentance is more than saying *I'm sorry*. It's turning around, changing direction, and walking back toward the One who loves us most. It's a spiritual exhale — that moment when the heaviness of guilt gives way to grace.

And Jesus says in Matthew 11:28, "Come to Me, all you who are weary and burdened, and I will give you rest." That's repentance — the invitation to rest in His mercy instead of wrestling with our regret.

Repentance doesn't remind us of how bad we are; it reminds us of how good God is. It's not about punishment — it's about peace. It's about laying down the heavy things and walking lighter, forgiven, and free.

When we hold onto sin, it holds onto us, pulling us down. But when we bring our burden to God, He doesn't just forgive — He restores.

✝

Takeaway:
Repentance isn't about shame — it's about surrender. Freedom begins the moment you stop carrying what God already paid to take from you.

Question for Reflection:
What burdens have you been carrying that God is inviting you to lay down in repentance today?

✝

Prayer:
Lord, I've carried some heavy things for far too long — guilt, regret, and moments I wish I could undo. But You never asked me to bear them alone. Today, I lay these burdens at Your feet. I repent for the ways I've fallen short and turn my heart back toward You. Thank You for meeting me not with condemnation but with compassion. Cleanse me, restore me, and help me walk lighter because of your grace and mercy. You have forgiven me and set me free. Amen.

✝

46. Living Free from Sin

"So if the Son sets you free, you will be free indeed." - *John 8:36 (NIV)*
"For all have sinned and fall short of the glory of God." - *Romans 3:23 (NIV)*
"For sin shall no longer be your master, because you are not under the law, but under grace." - *Romans 6:14 (NIV)*

———————————— † ————————————

Let's be honest — living free from sin feels impossible sometimes.

We're human. Flawed. Imperfect. Even after being rescued, redeemed, and walking with Jesus, we still trip and stumble. Sometimes we sin by our choice of words. Sometimes with our thoughts. Sometimes in what we fail to do when we know we should have done better.

For years, I thought "freedom from sin" meant reaching a perfect place where I never messed up again — that if I slipped or overlooked a step, I wasn't "doing Christianity right." But that's not what Jesus meant when He said, "If the Son sets you free, you will be free indeed."

Freedom from sin doesn't mean we'll never sin again, or worse, - it's OK to sin. No, it means sin no longer owns us. It doesn't control, define, or condemn us. Romans 6:14 says it clearly: "Sin shall no longer be your master."

Living free from sin is really about learning to live *freely* in a world full of sin — to walk through it without being ruled by it. Grace catches us when we fall, but it's not a "get out of guilt" card. God's grace doesn't give us permission to run wild; it gives us power to rise higher. Grace isn't a pass to live recklessly — it's the invitation to live righteously, unlocking the shackles holding us to our sins.

Freedom in Christ calls us to stay close to Him — to check our hearts often, to turn quickly when we realize we've strayed, and to let grace strengthen rather than excuse us.

This same type of freedom is mirrored in how a child learns to walk. The child may fall over and over, but they don't give up. Their parents don't scold them for falling — they help them up every single time until walking becomes second nature. That's what God does for us.

Freedom in Christ doesn't mean we never fall. It means that when we do, we fall into His grace, and then we get back up and keep walking.

Takeaway:
Grace isn't permission to sin — it's power to overcome it. Freedom in Christ means falling into God's grace, standing up stronger, and walking forward with purpose.

Question for Reflection:
Do you see God's grace as an excuse or as empowerment? What might change if you treated grace as a reason to grow instead of a reason to relax?

— ✝ —

Prayer:
Lord, thank You that Your grace isn't a free pass — it's a fresh start. Help me live responsibly in the freedom You've given me. When I stumble, remind me that Your grace lifts me, but also calls me higher. Teach me to walk wisely, love deeply, and reflect Your holiness — not out of obligation, but out of gratitude. Amen.

— ✝ —

47. Repentance as a Form of Surrender

"Humble yourselves, therefore, under God's mighty hand, that He may lift you up in due time." - *1 Peter 5:6 (NIV)*
"Create in me a pure heart, O God, and renew a steadfast spirit within me." - *Psalm 51:10 (NIV)*
"Submit yourselves, then, to God. Resist the devil, and he will flee from you." - *James 4:7 (NIV)*

———————————— † ————————————

Repentance isn't just an apology — it's an act of surrender.

It's the moment when we stop fighting for control and start handing it back to God. It's saying, "Lord, I'm done trying to fix this my way."

True repentance isn't about listing our mistakes — it's about opening our hearts and allowing God to transform what we've been trying to hide.

For me, repentance has often meant reaching the end of myself. When I've carried guilt for too long, when pride has tried to justify my choices, or when I've convinced myself I could manage my messes alone — that's when God gently whispers, "Will you let Me take it from here?"

Surrender happens when I stop trying to justify my actions, and instead hand my brokenness to the one who justifies by faith.

It's letting go of our own strength, our explanations, and our excuses. It's choosing humility over self-preservation and seeking honesty over pride.

Psalm 51:10 captures that beautifully: "Create in me a pure heart, O God, and renew a steadfast spirit within me." When David prayed those words, he wasn't just confessing his sin — he was offering his heart back to God for reshaping.

And 1 Peter 5:6 reminds us that when we humble ourselves before God, He will lift us up in due time. That's the beauty of surrender — we bow low so He can lift us high.

When I think about repentance as surrender, I picture kneeling at the edge of a battlefield. You've fought, struggled, and worn yourself out trying to justify your sin. But repentance is when you finally lay down the weapons — your pride, your defenses, your control — and raise your hands in surrender to the One who has been fighting for you all along.

The beautiful thing about God's kingdom is this: in surrender, we don't lose — we win.

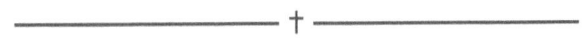

Takeaway:
Repentance isn't admitting defeat; it's receiving freedom. The moment you surrender your will to God, He trades your burden for His peace by forgiving you of your wrongs.

Question for Reflection:
What area of your life is God asking you to stop fighting and simply surrender?

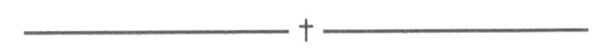

Prayer:
Lord, I've tried to handle so many things on my own — and I'm tired. Today, I choose to surrender all of myself to You. I lay down my pride, my guilt, and my need to be in control. Create in me a clean heart, and renew my spirit so I can walk in step with You. Help me remember that surrender isn't weakness — it's the doorway to Your strength. Amen.

48. Walking in Freedom, Not Condemnation

"Therefore, there is now no condemnation for those who are in Christ Jesus." - *Romans 8:1 (NIV)*

"If we confess our sins, He is faithful and just and will forgive us our sins and purify us from all unrighteousness." - *1 John 1:9 (NIV)*

"Forget the former things; do not dwell on the past. See, I am doing a new thing!" - *Isaiah 43:18–19 (NIV)*

———————— † ————————

There's a moment after repentance when silence falls — that strange space between forgiveness and freedom. You know God has forgiven you, yet the echoes of guilt linger in the back of your mind. You replay the words, the choices, the failures, whispering, *"How could God still love me after that?"*

But Romans 8:1 declares, "There is now no condemnation for those who are in Christ Jesus." None. Not *some*. Not *once you've proven yourself*. None.

Condemnation is the enemy's favorite counterfeit. Where conviction draws us closer to God, condemnation tries to drive us away. Conviction says, *"You messed up — come home."* Condemnation says, *"You messed up — stay gone."*

To walk in freedom is to choose which voice we listen to and believe.

For a long time, I confused humility with shame. I thought replaying my failures showed I was taking my sin seriously. But God never asked me to relive what He already released. Isaiah 43:18–19 reminds us, "Forget the former things; do not dwell on the past. See, I am doing a new thing!" God isn't stuck in your past — and you don't have to be either.

Walking in freedom is like a prisoner standing in an unlocked cell. The chains are gone, the door is open — but freedom still requires a choice: to leave the cell behind and step into the light.

1 John 1:9 promises that when we confess, God not only forgives but purifies us. He wipes the slate completely clean. Walking in freedom means refusing to pick up what Jesus already put down.

You don't have to earn your way back into God's favor. You're already there. You're already loved. You're already free. Leave the prison cell, the door is open and the way is clear.

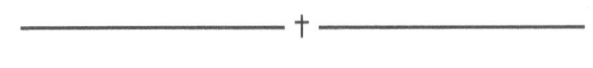

Takeaway:
Condemnation looks backward; freedom looks forward. You are not defined by what you did — you are defined by what Christ did for you.

Question for Reflection:
What memories or regrets keep you chained to a past that God has already forgiven? What would happen if you truly let them go and took your first steps in freedom?

✝

Prayer:
Lord, thank You that there is no condemnation for those who belong to You. Help me to walk boldly in the freedom You've given me — not looking back in shame, but forward in gratitude. Silence the voice of condemnation and let Your truth be louder. I choose to leave the cell behind and live as one who is free indeed.
Amen.

✝

49. Obedience

"If you love Me, keep My commandments." - *John 14:15 (NKJV)*
"To obey is better than sacrifice, and to heed is better than the fat of rams." - *1 Samuel 15:22 (NIV)*
"Trust in the Lord with all your heart and lean not on your own understanding; in all your ways submit to Him, and He will make your paths straight." - *Proverbs 3:5–6 (NIV)*

———————————— † ————————————

Boy, obedience is a tough one — let me tell you!

I often think of obedience as "obedience training" a puppy. The untrained puppy is always told to sit, stay, or heel by their master at the other end of a leash - and I think, *"Well, that sure doesn't sound like something I want to be part of! You can't tell me what to do!"*

And then came the day I settled on a "pet name" for God. I wanted something personal, something intimate between Him and me — so I just happened to choose one of the Hebrew names for God: *Adonai.* I liked the way it sounded, and it just felt *right.*

Later, I learned it not only means *Lord* — it also means *Master.* Imagine that…ME… calling someone *Master!*
That's proof that the Lord's got jokes!

But over time, I began to understand what obedience to the Lord really means — not as the world defines it, like my puppy example, but as Heaven does.

Obedience is not about being controlled or diminished. It's about surrender, commitment, and love. Obedience is an act of trust. It's saying, "Lord, I don't have to understand. I just have to follow."

When we obey God, we're not giving up freedom — we're walking into it.

You know what I find funny? People dream of being wealthy enough to have on-hand staff: a personal chef, housekeepers, gardeners, assistants — people to handle every detail so they can rest easy.

But when it comes to God — the One who actually knows how to handle every detail of our lives — we resist handing Him control!

We cling to our plans, our timing, our way, even when it's wearing us out. We say we trust Him, but we still keep one hand on the steering wheel of our lives *just in case*.

True obedience is letting go of every detail of our lives. It's realizing that *Adonai* doesn't demand obedience by yanking on a chain, He invites surrender through submitting our will to Him because we want to.

He's not looking for mindless robots; He's looking for real relationship.

The most peaceful place we can ever be is in total obedience to His will — because His will always leads to what's best for us, even when we think we know better in the moment.

When we finally stop resisting God and start following Him, we discover that obedience isn't about losing control or ourselves — it's about gaining peace and finding our purpose

Takeaway:
Obedience isn't punishment — it's partnership with the Lord. When you trust God enough to let Him lead, you discover His path was always safer, smoother, and sweeter than the one you tried to carve alone - even He takes you where you least expected.

Question for Reflection:
Where in your life is God asking you to surrender control — and what's holding you back from saying, "Yes, Lord, send me"?

---------------- † ----------------

Prayer:

Adonai, my Lord and my Master, teach me to walk in obedience with joy and humility. Help me trust that Your ways are higher than mine, and that surrender isn't weakness — it's wisdom. I give You the reins, the wheel, and every detail I've tried to control. Lead me in Your peace, and let my obedience be a reflection of my love for You. Amen.

---------------- † ----------------

50. Forgiveness

"Bear with each other and forgive one another if any of you has a grievance against someone. Forgive as the Lord forgave you." - Colossians 3:13 (NIV)

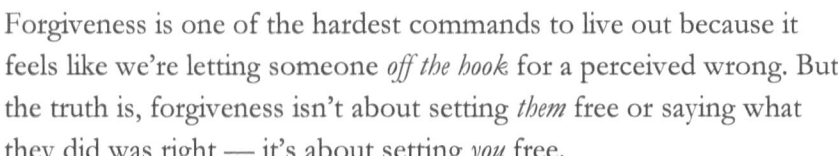

Forgiveness is one of the hardest commands to live out because it feels like we're letting someone *off the hook* for a perceived wrong. But the truth is, forgiveness isn't about setting *them* free or saying what they did was right — it's about setting *you* free.

When we hold onto unforgiveness, it becomes like a chain around our spirit, binding us to the very moment we were hurt. Our emotions are anchored in the past, unable to move forward.

We all have what I call our *"But…" closet*. It's that hidden space within us where we store the things we don't really want to let go of. We might tell ourselves we've forgiven someone — *but…* deep down, a small piece of the hurt still sits festering for the next time we think of the person who wronged us. You even retrieve that smoldering chunk of unforgiveness from the "But…" closet when you say things like:

"I forgive you for what you said about me, *but…* not for what you did."
"I forgive you for that moment, *but…* not for the pain it caused."

"I forgive you for your actions that one time, *but…* not this time."

That *"But…" closet* can fill up fast the unforgiveness junk. Every hurt we partially forgive becomes another box of rotten debris shoved onto the shelf, It becomes another weight quietly taking up space in our hearts, another chain anchoring us to a past hurt.

But... there's hope. True forgiveness happens when we finally open that door and hand every tattered box — every hidden hurt — to Jesus and let Him clean it all out.

Now, this doesn't mean what was done to us was okay. It simply means we're no longer carrying the burden of unforgiveness that came along with it. We're dropping those heavy stones of burden and letting the Lord deal with them. After all, I'd rather stock that closet with memories of how good God is, than place another box of grudges in there.

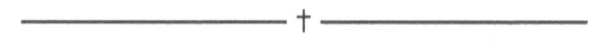

Takeaway:
You can't heal from the hurt you still have stored away. Empty your *"But..." closet* and trust Jesus to handle what you've been holding onto.

Question for Reflection:
What's hiding in your *"But..." closet* today? Are you ready to give it to God?

Prayer:
Lord, thank You for showing me the places in my heart where I've been holding back forgiveness. I don't want to keep a "But..." closet anymore. Help me release every hidden hurt and trust You with every wound. Teach me to forgive fully, freely, and without condition — just as You forgave me. Amen.

When You Need to Breathe Again

There comes a moment after the storms, the stretching, and the surrender when your soul simply needs to breathe again. Not to rush forward or look back — but to rest.

This isn't the breath of exhaustion; it's the breath of renewal. The kind that fills your lungs after a long climb, reminding you that you made it to the top — not by your strength, but by His.

Every tear, every trial, every turning point along the way has been leading you here — to stillness. To peace. To the quiet awareness that even when life is uncertain, *God is still steady*.

This final section isn't about striving; it's about settling. It's where you pause, inhale His presence, and exhale everything you were never meant to carry.

Because sometimes the holiest thing you can do… is *just breathe*.

———————————— † ————————————

Just Breathe

"The Lord will fight for you; you need only to be still." - *Exodus 14:14 (NIV)*
"...Be still, and know that I am God." - *Psalm 46:10 (NIV)*
"Come to Me, all you who are weary and burdened, and I will give you rest." - *Matthew 11:28 (NIV)*

---------------------------- † ----------------------------

Sometimes the most spiritual thing we can do is... *just breathe.*

We spend so much of life in motion — fixing, planning, working, worrying, praying, trying — that we forget the simple holiness of stillness. The sacred act of taking a deep breath, closing our eyes, and simply resting in the presence of the Lord.

Life can feel like a constant battle — with spiritual warfare, stress, heartache, responsibilities, expectations — and a never-ending swirl of noise and need. But in that chaos, God whispers one steady command:

Be still.

He doesn't need you to fix it all.
He doesn't need you to have the right words.
He just wants you to breathe — to pause long enough for Him to remind you that He's already fighting for you.

When you take that breath, it's more than oxygen. It's surrender. It's the soul exhaling fear and inhaling faith.

Psalm 46:10 says, *"Be still, and know that I am God."*
Stillness isn't the absence of movement; it's the awareness of presence — *His* presence.

"Just Breathe" is an invitation to lay it all down for a moment — the worries, the questions, the striving — and rest in the reality that God is here. Right here. Right now.

Exhale the tension.
Inhale His peace.
Exhale the doubt.
Inhale His grace.

You've walked through the fire and found victory on the other side. You've endured the storms and seen His restoration unfold. Now, this is your moment to simply breathe and *be*.

Because before you step back into the fray, before you take on another day, there's beauty in stillness — where the soul and Savior meet, and all is well.

———————— † ————————

Takeaway:
Inhale grace. Exhale control.
You don't have to hold everything together — the One who holds the universe already holds you.

Question for Reflection:
When was the last time you paused simply to breathe in God's presence? What might He be trying to whisper in that stillness?

———————— † ————————

Prayer:

Lord, thank You for the gift of breath — for the reminder that I don't have to rush or fix or strive. Teach me to find You in stillness. When life feels loud and heavy, help me to pause, breathe, and rest in Your presence. You are my peace, my renewal, and my quiet victory. Amen.

———————— † ————————

Epilogue: The Breath After the Battle

If you've made it here — to the final page — take a deep breath with me.

You did it. You walked through fifty devotions. Fifty reflections. Fifty moments where you chose to pause, listen, and let God meet you right where you were. And maybe, like me, you didn't arrive here the same way you started. Maybe you came carrying heaviness — guilt, fear, anger, or heartbreak. But along the way, piece by piece, you've learned to set it down.

When I first began writing *Lifted*, I didn't know that God would use it to heal so much inside of me, too. Each devotion was a mirror — sometimes a gentle reflection, sometimes a sharp smudge — showing me where He was still restoring what life had tried to break.

I've been rescued by Him. I've been refined because of Him. And through every fire, He's taught me how to breathe again.

If there's one thing I hope you carry from these pages, it's this: **you were never meant to do this life alone.**
Through every battle, every wilderness, every silent night — God has been there. Lifting you. Strengthening you. Loving you through the ache.

This devotional isn't just a collection of words — it's a journey of surrender and survival, of falling into the arms of grace again and again. And if I could sit across from you right now, coffee cup in hand, I'd tell you:

You're doing better than you think.
You're healing, even if it doesn't feel like it yet.
And God isn't finished with you — not by a long shot.

So breathe.
Let go.
Trust Him.

You don't have to have it all figured out — you just have to keep
showing up with an open heart. The same God who carried me out
of the darkest places will carry you too.

You are lifted.
You are loved.
And your story isn't over.
In fact... it's just beginning.

———————— † ————————

Closing Prayer

Heavenly Father,
Thank You for every person who has walked through these pages
with me — for every tear, every prayer, every whispered "help me"
that reached Your throne.
Thank You for rescuing us, for redeeming what the world tried to
destroy, and for teaching us that freedom isn't found in perfection —
it's found in Your presence.

As this journey closes, I pray it becomes a doorway to something
new — whether it's a deeper walk, a lighter heart, a steadier faith, or
even just a better relationship with You, Lord.
Let every person reading this feel Your nearness in their next breath.
Remind them that they are not forgotten, not forsaken, not finished,
and never alone.

May Your peace settle over them like morning light.
May Your Spirit breathe life into the places that still feel weary.
And may their hearts forever echo the truth that has carried me
through every chapter of my own story —
That You are faithful. You are good. And You never let go.

That YOU LIFTED!

In Jesus' mighty and merciful name,
Amen.

— ✝ —

Final Thanks

To my proofreaders, thank you for lending your time, your keen eyes, and your patient attention to detail in the final stages of this project. Your willingness to walk with me through every comma, correction, and clarification helped bring this book to its very best.

To the beautiful ladies of Kingdom Women, your unwavering love, encouragement, and faith have meant more to me than words could ever express. You have been my sisters, my cheerleaders, and my prayer warriors.

To the men and women of Celebrate Recovery, thank you for keeping me grounded, accountable, and connected when I was tempted to pull away. You reminded me that healing happens in community.

To Deb and Dave, your constant kindness, concern, and care—especially when my health falters—have been a steady light in difficult seasons. I am deeply grateful for your friendship and love.

To Anita, Todd, Bertie, and the gang, thank you for adopting me into your little clan and loving on me the way you have. You're the extended family I've always prayed for.

And finally, to every single person who picks up a copy of this book—thank you. Without you, these words would remain just ink on paper. Because of you, they become light. Thank you for allowing me to be your lighthouse for Christ.

— † —

This page intentionally left blank.